Your Inspiration Break

Words of Hope, Humor, and Healing

Lynn Jones

To: Blanche

May God bless and inspire you!

~Lynn Jones

Your Inspiration Break

Words of Hope, Humor, and Healing

Published by Austin Brothers Publishing, Fort Worth, Texas

www.abpbooks.com

ISBN 978-0-9996328-3-3

Printed in the United States of America
2018 -- First Edition

Dedicated to my wife Danielle,
who has shared my journey for fifty years,
has blessed my life and ministry
in more ways than I can count,
and who insisted that I ought to write a book.

Contents

Introduction

Some of our favorite words are, "Take a break!" "It's time for a coffee break!" Nothing is more beloved than break time. We take a break to rest and refresh our bodies. After taking a break, we can go back to our work and routines with renewed energy and effectiveness.

Something else that we need to do each day is to take an "Inspiration Break." We may grow weary or lose focus in our Christian lives. What we need to do at least a few minutes each day is to break for inspiration. If renewing our physical body is essential, it is even more important to replenish our souls.

This book is a collection of words of hope, humor, and healing that can inspire and help you each day. The "inspiration breaks" are not long. You can read each of them in a few minutes, but hopefully, they can be like the starter on your automobile. They can set some things in motion in your life that you can continue to think about, meditate on, and do throughout the day. Each "inspiration break" stands alone. You can read one or several each day. The "inspiration breaks" are a mixture of hope, humor, and healing for the hurts of life.

I grew up in Plainview, Louisiana, a small country community in West Central Louisiana. Plainview was not much to look it, but it was a wonderful place to look from. Some of the "inspiration breaks" come from my child-hood. Others come from the 54 years that I have spent as a pastor of nine churches in three different states. I have been blessed and inspired by many different people across these years. My prayer is that these "inspiration breaks" will inspire and help you!

A Life of Learning

A small boy came in the front door of his home after the first day of the new school year. His mother greeted him and asked the question that parents always ask. "Well, what did you learn at school today?"

The little boy responded, "All I learned was how to spell cat—k-a-t."

His mother said, "That's not how you spell cat."

He replied, "In that case, I didn't learn anything."

The first days of school are a mixture of excitement, anxiety, and new beginnings for everyone involved. I wonder if it was like that for Paul when he attended his first day of class in Jerusalem? Paul was not from Jerusalem originally. According to his testimony in Acts 22:3, he had been "born in Tarsus of Cilicia." He then came to Jerusalem and sat at the feet of Gamaliel as his student.

We learn by observing Paul that education is important. Some years ago, Robert Fulghum wrote a little essay that later became the title of his first book: All I Really Need to Know I Learned in Kindergarten. The essay made a valid point that certain attitudes and understandings which we use all of our lives are learned in kindergarten. But in a strict sense, the title is not accurate. We did not learn all we needed to know while we were in kindergarten. We live in a complex world that challenges us always to be going farther in our education.

Paul sat at the feet of Gamaliel until he was a young man, and then he left that school. He did not, however, leave learning. For the rest of his life, he continued to read, study, and explore. One of the most touching passages in one of his letters is found in 2 Timothy 4:13. Writing from his prison cell in Rome, near the end of his life, he said to Timothy, "Bring the cloak that I left with Carpus at Troas when you come—and the books, especially the parchments." He was nearing the end of his life, but he still had an insatiable desire to learn. He was a student all of his life.

That is our need as well. Education is not something you've got. It's something you're always getting. I encourage you to stay with the books. If you're not a reader, I encourage you to keep your eyes open and your antennae up and look for other ways of gaining knowledge.

Some of the most profound, life-changing lessons are learned outside the classroom. Paul had been an "A" student, but he was a failure when it came to the most critical lesson in life—the need to acknowledge Jesus Christ as his Savior and Lord. It was not until his journey to Damascus. It was not in a classroom that he learned the lesson. It was on the road. It is the lesson of ultimate importance that everyone needs to learn.

Becoming Strong

When I was a boy, on most Saturdays, we went from Plainview, Louisiana, to Many, Louisiana, to shop. For me, the highlight of the day was going to Morgan and Lindsey Variety Store. Mom would give me a dime, and I would buy a comic book. I wanted to read the comic book on the way home, but I always got car sick while reading. I would try to read a few pages and then had to stop until I got home.

On the back of a lot of the comic books was an ad showing muscleman Charles Atlas. Charles Atlas had at one time been a 90-pound weakling. A picture on the back showed him as a 90-pound weakling on the beach when a bully came by and kicked sand on him right in front of his girlfriend. It was very embarrassing! But Charles Atlas discovered the secret of "Dynamic Tension," and, by using this body building technique, he soon became a muscle man who never took anything from another bully.

It was not clear exactly what "Dynamic Tension" was, but, judging from the picture on the back of the comic book, it consisted of pushing with one arm against the other until you built bulging muscles. We were encouraged to fill out a coupon printed on the back of the comic book, send it to Charles Atlas, and he would show us the secrets of "Dynamic Tension."

We didn't have any beaches around Plainview, and I didn't have a girlfriend, but I sure didn't want to be embarrassed by some bully kicking sand on me in front of some future girlfriend, so I filled out the coupon and mailed it to Charles Atlas. On the coupon, you had to list your age, so in that blank, I put my age, "7." I was very disappointed that I never heard anything from Charles Atlas. He evidently thought that, given my age, I was a poor prospect for getting any money out of me.

It was quite a disappointment. Who knows what might have happened had I learned the secrets of "Dynamic Tension." I might have been whipping bullies on beaches all over the world. I might have been a member of the Power Team, breaking concrete blocks with my bare hands. But, it was not to be. I grew up to be a 145-pound weakling who studiously avoided beaches and bullies. But, it's really not my fault. You can lay all of the blame at the feet of one Charles Atlas!

Actually, the model for growth and strength is not Charles Atlas. It is Jesus Christ. Jesus "grew and became strong; he was filled with wisdom, and the grace of God was upon him" (Luke 2:40). Unfortunately, I have not become like Charles Atlas or Jesus, but my goal now is to become more like Jesus!

Shade in a Hot, Dry Land

Summer often brings a lot of heat and drought. Of course, West Texas is famous for those kinds of conditions. I heard about two ranchers who were visiting one day. One said to the other, "I'm a little concerned about my son. He is seven years old and still believes in Santa Claus."

"That's nothing," the other said, "My son is eight, and he still believes in rain."

A visitor to West Texas one summer was overwhelmed by how dry it was. She asked an old rancher if it ever rained out here. "Yes it does," he said. Then he added, "Do you remember Noah's flood? We got a half-inch that time."

Heat and drought make jobs tougher and patience shorter. A pastor came upon a boy who, in the hottest part of the day, was loading hay on a wagon with a pitchfork. The pastor felt sorry for the boy and told him that he ought to take a break. The boy said, "I'd better not. My daddy wouldn't like it."

The pastor said, "I'll talk to him about it. Where is he?" The boy said, "He's under this pile of hay."

Israel was an arid land. The heat and drought were realities with which the people had to cope. God's promises are often made against that backdrop. Isaiah pointed to a day when God would place a canopy over His people. He added, "It will be a shelter and shade from the heat of the day, and a refuge and hiding place from the storm and rain" (Is. 4:6). Isaiah expressed his praise to God: "You have been a refuge for the poor, a refuge for the needy in his distress, a shelter from the storm and a shade from the heat" (Is. 25:4). He pointed to a golden day in the future for God's people when "They will neither hunger nor thirst, nor will the desert heat or the sun beat upon them. He who has compassion on them will guide them and lead them beside springs of water" (Is. 49:10). You are invited to come and find rest in the shadow of His presence!

A Fellowship of Encouragement

Down home, a man decided to go into business for himself. He had always wanted to have his own sawmill, so when he had the opportunity, he bought a small one, moved it near his home, and was soon in business. He carried his old mule over to help pull some of the heavier loads around the mill. He also hired three men to help him run the mill.

With high hopes, he and his mule would head to the mill every morning to meet the three men who were working for him. All day long they cut ties and lumber. For three months, the mill was a beehive of activity. Then one day a neighbor passed by to see the mill idle. Concerned about the shutdown, the neighbor visited with the owner to ask what had happened.

The owner of the mill explained. He said, "Well, at the end of the three months I sat down to figure up how I was doing. I figured up all of my income and all of my expenses. That's when I discovered something. The only two at that mill who weren't getting paid were that mule and me."

In order for any of us to continue in an enterprise, we have to have some return on the investment. That return doesn't have to be monetary, but it does have to be something that we value—affirmation, a sense of accomplishing something of value, a sense of doing something important, or some other return. When that return is not felt, then discouragement is the order of the day.

How can the church help? The church can be a fellowship where we can jumpstart each other if one is low. We can be a fellowship of encouragement.

In a basketball game, you will see the player who scores a basket after receiving a pass always point to the person who made the pass. It is a way of expressing gratitude and encouragement. John Wooden, the longtime coach at UCLA, used to encourage his players to do that. One of his players asked, "Coach, what if you point to the player and he's not looking at you?" Wooden responded, "Don't worry, he'll be looking." Everyone hungers for appreciation and affirmation.

We can provide that appreciation and affirmation. We can be a fellowship of encouragement. The writer of Hebrews urged, "Let us not give up meeting together, as some are in the habit of doing, but let us encourage one another—and all the more as you see the Day approaching" (Heb. 10:25).

Fibber

What is your first memory? My first memory is of some dogs. It was shortly before my third birthday on June 10, 1948, when our dog Queen had puppies under the front porch of our house. Our house was on a conventional foundation, sitting on piers and beams, and the front porch was high off the ground. I remember crawling under that front porch (probably with my older brother Wayne) and seeing those little puppies with their mother. It was fitting that this should be my first memory because so much of my growing up was marked by an endless procession of dogs that came to our farm and crossed the path of my life. But, there was no other dog like one of them.

My dad was a hunter, and he wanted to train one of those puppies that were part of my first memory to be a good coon dog. (I know that the correct word is "raccoon," but nobody in Plainview ever said "raccoon." When it came to pronouncing words, we always took the easiest way out, and "coon" was so much easier to say than "raccoon). So, my dad picked out a male and female from the litter and kept them. In those days before television, my dad and mom's favorite show on the radio was the comedy, "Fibber McGee and Molly." So, my dad named those two puppies "Fibber" and "Molly." (Daddy always had catchy names for his dogs through the years. In honor of the astronaut, Gus Grisson, who died in an accident in the early days of space exploration, he named one of his dogs "Gus." At other times, he gave pairs of dogs catchy names. He had two that he called "Shag" and "Shine," and two that he called "Nip" and "Tuck.") But there was never another dog on our farm like Fibber. Molly fell by the wayside, but Fibber became Daddy's pride and joy and, in the opinions of many, chief of whom was my dad, he became the best coon dog in the country.

People came from all over the country to hunt with him and my dad. And when the coons were eating the corn in people's fields and gardens in the summertime, Daddy and Fibber were gone almost every night to hunt the offending coons. "Fib," as he was affectionately called, (Remember, I told you that we always took the easy way out when it came to pronouncing words) was not strictly a coon dog. He would tree squirrels for us, chase cows off the front "stomp," and even chase a deer or a fox in a tight. But, preeminently, he was a coon dog. His two long ears became slit all around the edges by many hard-fought battles with coons so that they looked like the fringe on a lady's shawl. He would wade through brush, tree a coon, wait patiently for the hunters to arrive at the tree, fight the coon if they knocked it out of the tree, and then be off to find and tree other coons before the night was over.

Gradually, over the years, Fib and Daddy both got too old and disabled to hunt coons, but that never stopped them from recounting the glory years of their adventures together—Daddy by telling the story and Fib by whimpering in his dreams as he recalled ferocious fights in his past.

When Fibber died, we felt that a dog that had been such a big part of our lives needed a decent burial, so we carried his body down into the field, placed it between the graves of our paint horse "Calico" and Rickey's turtle "Herman," and buried him. We scratched his name, "Fib," into a piece of sandstone and placed it at the head of his grave.

On a farm, you come to know a lot of animals, and you respect them and their contributions to your life. It was only fitting that a dog that played such a significant role in my growing up, and whose birth was such an important event that it forms my very first memory, should have a place in our pet cemetery with his own headstone, "Fib," lovingly inscribed on it. There have been many other dogs in my life, but there has never been another one like "Fibber." I don't know about you, but I thank the Lord for everything that has blessed and enriched my life—and that includes a dog named "Fibber."

A Hovercraft Faith

In the fall of 1992, while I was pastor of Highland church in Shreveport, I had the opportunity to go to Hong Kong. In those years leading up to the return of Hong Kong to China, the Louisiana Baptist Convention had a partnership with Hong Kong Baptists. As part of that partnership, several teams of Louisiana Baptists went to Hong Kong to lead revivals and Christian growth clinics.

For two weeks, several of us had the opportunity to share the gospel in Hong Kong. It was a great experience. I enjoyed the opportunities to minister and to see that part of the world. During our time there, I took two side trips. On one of these, we crossed over from Hong Kong to a small port on the southern coast of China and then went to visit Canton (or, Guangzhou, as it is called now). On another trip, we crossed the same body of water to go to Macao. I carried some medicine to one of our mission-ary doctors in what was then a Portuguese colony.

One of the interesting things about both of these trips was that we made them by hovercraft. A hovercraft is a unique boat that actually hovers on the surface of the wa-ter. Giant fans force air down onto the water's surface so that it forms a cushion between the boat and the water. The craft does not churn the water; it skims on the wa-ter's surface. Since the boat does not encounter much re-sistance, it can travel very fast across the water's surface.

In some ways, many travel through life like a hov-ercraft. They never get beneath the surface. They just skim across the surface of life. The artist Andy Warhol summed up that approach to life. He said, "I am a deep-ly superficial person." Unfortunately, that paradoxical phrase could describe different dimensions of our lives. We become "deeply superficial."

Consider the area of our relationships with other peo-ple. We are often profoundly superficial. We are afraid to open up with others and to share anything more than on a superficial level. We skim along the surface with polite exchanges and don't share on deeper levels of life.

Or, you take our Christian life. After coming to know Christ as Savior, unfortunately, we often skim along the surface with Him. So many things beckon us to go deeper. We need to grow in our devotional lives. We need to ex-plore the depths of His Word. We need to come to deep-er understandings of our beliefs. Instead of doing so, we often settle for what Earnest Campbell called a "fortune cookie theology."

On one occasion, Jesus issued a challenge to Peter along the shore of the Sea of Galilee. He said to Peter, "Put out into deep water, and let down the nets for a catch" (Luke 5:4). Peter resisted, but when he finally followed that instruction, he caught a huge number of fish.

That's what we need to do. We need to quit skimming the surface and go into the deep water to let down our nets. We must not settle for a hovercraft faith!

Balking

When I was pastor of First Baptist Church in Booneville, each Monday, Wednesday, and Friday at 8:00 AM, I taught either New Testament Survey or Old Testament Survey at Northeast Mississippi Community College. Immediately after I finished with the classroom, I turned it over to Ray Scott who taught Baseball Theory. Sometimes when I came in to teach my class, a couple of days later I ran across some of Ray's notes on the board. Several times in the first part of the semester I ran across this line on the board: "Thirteen ways to balk."

That line intrigued me. In baseball, a "balk" is an illegal motion made by the pitcher when a runner is on base. I never had thought much about a "balk" until I saw that line on the board. I never dreamed that there were 13 ways of doing it. When I asked Ray about it, he gave me a printout with the 13 ways that a pitcher can balk. I would list all 13 for you, but I don't have room for them. In addition to that, I'm not sure that anyone has a burning desire to know the 13 ways to balk.

When I was growing up on the farm, we didn't play much baseball. Whenever we used the word "balk," we used it differently. We sometimes used "balk" to refer to a ridge of dirt between two furrows that had been plowed in the field. Or, more often, we used it to describe what a horse sometimes did. When a horse refused to go somewhere you wanted him to go, we said that he "balked."

We had an old plow horse named "Red Mare" that I occasionally tried to ride. Whenever I tried to ride her, she cooperated just enough to get the feed I offered as a bribe. Beyond that, she treated me with utter contempt. When I was riding her, she hated to cross a wooden bridge. When she came to a bridge, she would often refuse to cross it, and I didn't have enough authority to make her do it. She would "balk" on me.

Sometimes people "balk" on the Lord. For instance, the Lord told Jonah to go to Nineveh and preach to the city. Jonah refused to go. He "balked" on the Lord. Instead of going to Nineveh, he went in the opposite direction and boarded a ship for distant Tarshish. The Lord didn't take kindly to Jonah's refusal and had to enroll him in a short course in a fish's belly in the bottom of the sea before he began to see the wisdom of going in the direction God wanted him to go.

In the Book of Acts, God instructed Ananias to go talk to Paul in Damascus. Ananias initially balked at carrying out God's assignment until God explained about Paul's great encounter with the Lord on the road to Damascus.

A father said that his 6-year-old son got a dog for Christmas. He said, "We plan to send him to obedience school. If it works on him, we are also going to send the dog."

God does not take kindly to our "balking" on Him and His instructions. He has a way of sending us to obedience school in life. How do you respond to His directions for your life?

Big Decisions

A friend once asked me this question: "What are the ten most destructive decisions that a young person can make?" I gave the matter some thought. Out of my own experience and the experience of working with many young people over the years, it seems to me that these are the ten most destructive decisions a young person can make: (1) I will reject any belief in God. (2) I will regard all truth as being totally subjective. (3) I will pursue a vocation that pays well even if I detest the work. (4) I can use alcohol and drugs but won't get hooked like others. (5) I am young and can live recklessly because I don't have to worry about my health or safety. (6) I will coast through my educational years now and learn later. (7) I will marry this person without ever giving the long-term relationship serious thought. (8) I will reject anything associated with my past. (9) I will make all decisions based on "what's in it for me?" (10) I will buy on credit without any thought of paying it off.

I'm not sure what my list would have been if I had been asked the same question when I was 18. I'm sure that it would have been entirely different. It would have been different because experience and a changing perspective helps you to see some things as more important and some things as less important than you did when you were eighteen.

A boy was playing in a barn when he saw an old-fashioned yoke. It was heavy, but he found he could lift it. So he carried it out into the barnyard where he put one end of it over the head of a calf. Then, to add to the fun, he put his own head through the other end. This was more fun for him than for the calf. The calf let out a bellow and began running across the barnyard, dragging the boy with him. Hanging onto the yoke with all his strength to keep from being strangled, the boy yelled at the top of his voice, "Somebody catch us! We're running away!"

It's pretty easy to get yoked into something that turns out quite differently from what you expected. Sometimes it takes you farther, keeps you longer, and costs you more than you anticipated.

A far better decision that one can make is to step into the yoke with Jesus. You'll never find a better partner. To enter into partnership with Him is life's most productive decision.

Running Away from Home

When my younger brother Rick was born in 1948, I was three years old. I felt about his arrival like the little girl did who was asked how she felt about the addition to her family of a younger brother. She said, "He's okay, but there were a lot of other things that we needed worse."

Rick, was okay, but he wasn't much fun to play with when he was a baby. In order to take care of him while my mom was teaching school, my grandmother, whom we called "Mam-a," moved in with us. The next year, when I was four, Rick still wasn't able to play with me much, and time weighed heavy on my hands. One day, my mom said that maybe sometime at the end of a school day, I could come to school and ride the school bus to my cousin Lavelle's house. I could play with him for a while, and then she could come pick me up. Now, that sounded exciting, and, typical of kids, I understood that this was to happen the next day. When I told my grandmother about it the next day, she didn't know anything about it, and she refused to let me go to school to ride the bus that afternoon. I went out back of our house and cried and cried because she wouldn't let me go.

Finally, I decided to take matters into my own hands. I went into the clothes closet and found a pair of clean overalls and a clean shirt. Even though they had not been ironed, I put them on and headed out the back door, crossed the stile on the fence, and began running across our back field. My grandmother noticed that I was missing and began calling to me as I ran across the field. I pretended that I didn't hear her and ran faster.

By the time I reached the road that ran behind our field, our neighbor, Irene Cabra, had heard Mam-a calling me and said to me, "Lynn, your Mam-a is calling you."

I said, "I know it," and kept running. I ran through the sand bed in front of Plainview Baptist Church and made it to school just as it was dismissing. I dodged my mother who was somewhere around there, found my cousin Janis Cole, and announced that I was going to ride the bus home with her. She seemed only mildly surprised, and invited me to come on board.

It was fun riding the bus and even more fun arriving at the Cole's house. When the kids got home from school, Aunt Fourthie didn't have any Ding Dongs or Twinkies to give them, but she did have biscuits, and that's what she gave us that day. You took the biscuit, stuck your thumb into the side of it to make a hole, and then filled the hole with syrup. No Ding Dong ever tasted better.

After the biscuit and syrup, Lavelle and I had a big time—until my mother arrived with a perturbed look on her face and put an end to our fun. I thought I might be off the hook with her because I saw Aunt Fourthie and her smiling a little as she recounted what had happened that day. My hopes were soon dashed as she put me in the truck for the ride home. Along the way, I got a lecture on the seriousness of what I had done that day. I had scared my grandmother to death, and I had put myself in grave danger of being kidnapped or run over by a car. (Actually, nobody was ever kidnapped in Plainview nor run over by a car, but mothers know how to spin these things to their advantage.)

I had heard the story of the prodigal son in the Bible, and, since my mother was a God-fearing woman who went to church every Sunday, I entertained some hope that she would welcome me home by killing the fatted calf and having a party with music and dancing with all of my friends. When I arrived home, I could tell that the fatted calf had not been killed, and I immediately began making preparations for my own demise.

Mother got the belt from Daddy's closet, and that's when I went into my defensive posture. I began crying, promising that I would never do it again, and, as the punishment was being inflicted, I yelled as though I were being killed. I was not sincere about any of this, but I had learned from many similar experiences before then that it had a way of inflicting guilt upon my mother and short- ening the period of time that the punishment was being administered.

Finally, the worst was over, and I was told to "straight- en myself up" and get ready for supper. After hurrying through a very awkward supper, I went out back and thought about the day. It had been the first (and, as far as I can remember, the last) time that I had ever run away from home. It was such an exciting day that I have always remembered it. And, like most days, it had brought both pain and its pleasure.

Be Careful What You Teach Your Children

I have a confession to make—when I turn on a faucet, I have a hard time remembering whether the hot water is on the left side or the right side. But, it's not my fault. It'is entirely my brother Rick's fault. I was about five years old, and Rick was about two before we got indoor plumbing. In the late 1940's, electricity came to our farm in Plainview. Before that, water had to be drawn by hand, heated on the stove, and poured into a washtub in the kitchen where we took our baths. But, with the advent of electricity, everything changed. By putting an electric pump into our well, we now had the luxury of having running water at all times, an indoor bathroom, and a hot-water heater.

My mom didn't see this as an unmixed blessing. She could spot something dangerous from a mile away, and she immediately was gripped by fear over this new addition to our house. With Rick's running around the house as a two-year-old and hot water present in the bathroom with just a turn of the faucet, she envisioned his turning on the hot-water, putting himself under the faucet, and being scalded to death.

She wasn't worried about the hot water in the sink or the lavatory because Rick couldn't reach that, but the hot water faucet in the bathtub was different. It was low, reachable, and dangerous. I never did figure out how a two-year-old who didn't like to take baths anyway would go into the bathroom, turn the hot water on in the bathtub, and let it run all over his body enough to scald himself, but my mom had it figured out, and it haunted her.

As the bathroom was being installed, she worried about it constantly, so she came up with a solution. She had the plumber put the hot water faucet on the right side against the wall so that Rick couldn't reach it. That solved the immediate problem, and Rick grew up safely and soundly without ever once scalding himself.

The inversion of the faucets, however, had an unintended consequence. In my young, impressionable mind, it was imprinted deep into my subconscious circuitry that the hot water is on the right and the cold water is on the left. It was so deeply imprinted into my subconscious mind that now, more than 68 years later, whenever I go to turn on a faucet, I have to think through whether I am standing at our bathtub faucets in the old house or at the lavatory faucets. Sometimes, to this day, I still mess up and turn on the hot water when I mean to turn on the cold. It is another of a long list of things in my life that I blame on my younger brother!

Parents have to be careful about this sort of thing. What you are teaching your children at a young, impressionable age is going to stay with them. Teach them well!

Composting the Past

For many years, I saved all the leaves and grass clippings from my yard and turned them into compost. Then I used this to grow shrubs and flowers the next year. Eugene Peterson said that life is like that. Nothing from our past is thrown out with the garbage. It's all composted and assimilated into a growing life.

All of us are products of our pasts. When his friend James Thurber died, E. B. White paid tribute to Thurber's boyhood in Ohio. He said, "Ohio was never far from his thoughts, and when he received a medal from his home state in 1953, he wrote, 'The clocks that strike in my dreams are often the clocks of Columbus.'" The clocks that strike in our souls are often the clocks of our past. They have a tremendous influence on us.

Our pasts are a blend of both the difficult and the delightful. Telling the difference between the two often takes time. Have you ever noticed that Nobel prizes for scientific research are often awarded for work that was done years ago? One of the reasons for this is that it often takes time to realize the full impact of such research. At the time the results of the research were published, some may have paid little attention. It is only from the perspective of time that we realize that this was a monumental breakthrough. That's the way it is as we contemplate our pasts. It is only in retrospect that we see how some events have impacted our lives.

Another thing about this blend of events is that sometimes we want a repeat of what was good. We long, and maybe even pray, for the "good old days." C. S. Lewis said that that is the one prayer that God won't answer—a prayer for an encore. God's creativity is too vast for that. He is not some mindless projectionist who keeps showing the same scenes over and over. Lewis said that God won't give us the "good old days," but He will give us some "good new days."

Bell Cows

When I was growing up in Plainview, Louisiana, a lot of people had big herds of cattle. Most of these people didn't have pastures large enough to support these herds, but there was open range in the area, so they let their cows out to roam and feed on timber company land and government land.

One of the problems with this was that the cows often roamed far and wide, and it was hard to keep up with them. To solve this problem—enter the cowbell. In this part of Mississippi, cowbells are used primarily to identify and keep up with the fans of Mississippi State sports, but around home in those days not many people had ever heard of Mississippi State, but everyone was very familiar with cowbells.

To keep track of their roaming herds of cattle, the owners of these herds would identify one or two older cows that were natural leaders of the herd. When the owners had the cows up in their pasture, they would put a leather strap around the necks of these cows and attach cowbells to them. These cows were called "bell cows." When the bell cows had been outfitted with the cowbells, these leaders of the herd would lead the cows out to graze. When you were looking for your cows, you could listen carefully and hear the sound of these bells for a long way. When you followed the sound of the bells, it would lead you to the bell cows, and the rest of the herd would be right behind them.

When I was pastor of Central Baptist Church in Springhill, Louisiana, Bro. Walter Barnard was a member of our church. Bro. Walter was a retired Director of Missions and was still very active in associational affairs. When he was sponsoring a meeting or some program, he would often say to me, "Now I want you to talk to some of those old bell cows in your church and get them behind this program and this project."

Of course, he was talking about some of the natural leaders in the church. Bro. Walter had learned a lesson that every pastor has to learn. It was that identifying "bell cows" and learning to work with them is a key to being effective in a church.

Like it or not, there are natural leaders that emerge in every church. Some of these "bell cows" are a bit defensive and territorial about their positions Some are like the old doctor who was retired. As patients were sitting in the waiting room to see a doctor, they heard a man shouting, "Tetanus, flu, pneumonia."

A nurse said to the patients in the waiting room, "Don't pay any attention to him. He's a doctor who is now retired but used to practice here. He still likes to come in and call the shots."

Not every leader is like that. Others are very open and cooperative. In working with these leaders, when we are creative, loving, and willing to build bridges and draw bigger circles, we can usually avoid confrontations that are harmful to the church and forge relationships that are helpful and redemptive. May God bless the "bell cows" that give leadership, and may He bless those who follow and work with them to get the church where it needs to be.

Taking a Detour

Herb Dickerson is a good friend of mine. Herb has served as a pastor, seminary teacher, and director of missions for the past 50 years. I first got to know Herb when I was serving as pastor of Herb's home church, Burkeville Baptist Church in Burkeville, Texas. Burkeville is a village about 10 miles southwest of the dam on Toledo Bend Reservoir in Southeast Texas.

When Herb was in high school at Burkeville, he lived about four miles south of town, down County Road 1414. That distance from the school became a problem for him at times because he didn't have a car and loved to play basketball. When the high school basketball team came in from an "away" game late at night, he couldn't always count on somebody giving him a ride home. Faced with that situation, he had no choice but to walk the four miles down 1414 to his house.

Herb was young and in good shape, but there was a significant problem that he faced when had to walk home late at night. Mr. Oza Hall lived on 1414 before you got to Herb's house, and Mr. Oza had a lot of cows that came up at night and slept on the road in front of his house. Most of them were no threat, but there was one exception to that. Mr. Oza had one big bull that slept on the road and getting past him was a problem. Herb said that he began worrying about that bull every time that he started his walk down 1414 late at night. Mr. Oza's house was located just about half a mile before Herb would reach his own house, so the location of the house and the threatening bull were problems—they came at a point in Herb's trip when he was most tired and the night was the darkest. Outrunning that bull, should he charge him at that point in his journey, would be a big problem given Herb's fatigue and the darkness of the night.

So, after walking three and one-half miles, Herb would approach Mr. Oza's place with great caution. He would slow his walk until he was barely creeping. When he got close enough to see if the cows and the big bull were sleeping in the road that night, he knew what he had to do. If the cows and the big bull were blocking the road, Herb would veer off the road and into the thick, dark woods. He would tromp his way through thickets and stump holes for about a quarter of a mile until he came out on 1414 well past the big bull. It delayed his arrival at home and led to scratches, mosquito bites, and sometimes a load of seed ticks, but it was worth it. Scratches, mosquitoes, and seed ticks won't kill you, but a big bull can. Herb has always been smart about things like that.

You don't always need to hit things head-on. If you meet a bull or some other big obstacle that is in your path, the best course of action is to take a detour around it. It may be a little more difficult in the short haul, but in the long haul, it will save you (and your surviving family members) a lot of grief!

Blackberry Picking

When I was a boy, one of our annual rituals was picking blackberries. Mom would give each of us boys a bucket and march us off to do battle with the blackberries. On the briars growing around our fencerows and in the woods beyond, we always had plenty of blackberries. Picking blackberries was not easy, however. In those days before insect repellant had been invented, I often got more redbugs (people in other parts of the world call them chiggers, but we never used that word in Plainview) than blackberries.

In their tiny little insect brains, the redbugs had figured things out. They knew that when the blackberries got ripe that a lot of warm-blooded animals would be making their way to the blackberry vines, so they situated themselves on the vines next to the best berries and waited. Sure enough, my brothers and I showed up every year, and they were always ready to take full advantage of us. Not only was there the threat of the redbugs, but also the briars would scratch you, and the berries were small—it would take all morning to fill a bucket.

On top of all that, after you had picked blackberries all morning, you didn't get to eat many of them. Mom wanted to "take them away" from us when we were through. You had to fight your natural tendency to hold onto them. But, if you were willing to give them up to her, she would do all kinds of good things with them. If you allowed her to have them, those berries would come back to you in a far more wonderful way than when you gave them up. Sometimes, she would give them back to you with sugar and cream on them. Or, she would give them back to you as blackberry jelly and jam served on the tops of big biscuits on cold mornings. Or, sometimes they came back to you in the form of blackberry cobbler with ice cream on top. If you were willing to give them to her, they always came back better than when you let them go.

And God can do that with the good and the bad things in your life. If you are willing to take what you have, the good and the bad, and give it to God, He can take it all and make it better. Don't hold onto life. Give it up to God and allow Him to make it better!

Breaking into the Pastor's Study

While I was pastor of Highland Baptist Church in Shreveport, LA, we kept the doors locked during the week and had a camera, intercom, and automatic unlock feature that the secretaries could use when someone came to the door. In spite of these security features, some folks would occasionally slip into the building for purposes other than a desire to worship the Lord.

One day after lunch, I came back to my office, which was on the second floor. I sat down at my desk and was working on some papers when I thought I saw something move on the other side of my desk. I looked up, and I saw the back of a man who had stooped down on the other side of my desk. I didn't say anything. I just got up as quietly as I could and left the office and went downstairs.

As I reached the bottom of the stairs, I heard him come out of the office behind me and start running down the upstairs hallway in the opposite direction. When I went into the hallway on the first floor, I saw our two custodians at the opposite end of the hallway. I told them that a man would probably be coming down the stairway on their end of the hall. About that time, the intruder burst through the door into the hallway. When he saw two large custodians on that end of the hallway and one small preacher on the other end of the hallway, he started running in the direction of the one small preacher. As he came toward me, I yelled, "Stop," and then I stood in front of the exit door and took the position of an NFL lineman defending a quarterback from an onrushing defensive tackle. The man running at me doubled up his fist and headed for the door and me. Just before he reached me, I jumped to the side like a matador and let him exit the building.

It was a very unnerving experience. When I finally settled down, I went back up to my office to see if he had taken anything. I couldn't find anything missing. The only thing that I could figure was that he had probably heard of my preaching and had broken into my office to read some of my sermons! Who would have thought that there would ever be such a demand for them? The good news is that you don't have to break into your pastor's study to read his sermons. He will be offering them in oral form for free next Sunday. I encourage you to go hear him.

Churches That Work

Two men were talking about their churches. One said to the other, "Well, I'll tell you one thing about our church—on resurrection day our church will be the first one out of the grave."

The other said defensively, "Oh yeah? What makes you think so?"

"Because," the man said, "the Bible says that the dead in Christ shall rise first."

Keeping the church alive and vital has always been a challenge. That involves keeping everyone involved in the life and ministry of the church.

Someone has estimated that in the typical church about 15% of the people are involved in active service. The other 85% can be divided into three groups: The spectators, the cheerleaders, and the critics. The spectators observe impassively. The cheerleaders don't do any work, but they are happy to cheer on those who do. The critics not only don't do any work, but they are critical of those who do. If you had to place yourself into one of these categories, which one would it be?

If the church is going to accomplish its purpose, it needs all its members to do their part. I read about a newspaper editor who called two reporters into his office. He told them that he wanted them to go out and cover a breaking story. He had received word that there was an electrical power line down on a busy city street. Reports were unclear about whether electrical power was still in the downed line. One of the reporters asked the editor why he was sending two of them out on the story. He responded, "I want one of you to touch the power line and the other one to write the story."

Effective churches require persons who are willing to do many different jobs. Some of the jobs receive a lot of attention. Others will never be noticed. Good churches are filled with people who are willing to do all kinds of jobs. What kind of job are you willing to do in the church?

Confessing Our Faith

I heard of a wife who asked her husband, "Are we out of the woods financially yet?' He replied,

"Yes, we are out of the woods. But now we are in the quicksand."

That is the case with many people today. They are continually moving from one financial crisis to another. Sometimes this crisis is produced by the headlong rush to plug the empty places in our lives with things. A cartoon showed two women coming out of a department store with huge sacks of purchases in their hands. One was saying to the other, "Whoever said that money can't buy happiness doesn't know where to shop."

The quest to consume constantly puts persons in financial jams. In spite of that, many find it difficult to exercise discipline in this area of their lives. A husband said to his wife, "I have figured out a solution to our financial dilemma. If we miss two payments on the refrigerator and one on the washing machine, we will have enough for a down payment on a new television."

One of the problems with this kind of financial over-commitment is that persons often have little money to give to the Lord's work. One man told a friend that on the night before he had had a terrible nightmare. He said, "I dreamed that my income was ten times the amount of my tithe." He added, "I was so poor that I had to borrow money from my brother-in-law to buy shoestrings."

Does the Bible have anything to say about how we use our money? The answer is, "Yes!" The Bible has a great deal to say about money, our attitudes toward it, and our stewardship of it. We confess our faith in many ways. One of the ways that we need to do it is in the stewardship of our financial resources.

Costless Christianity?

It was not until about 1948 that electricity arrived at our house in Plainview, Louisiana. One of my first memories is seeing the men put those big poles into the ground and stringing the wires that would bring this miracle energy source to the place where we lived. The advent of electricity opened up all kinds of possibilities for labor-saving devices. I didn't care much about such items, but my mom did. Loaded with a full-time teaching job and three boys under the age of eight, she needed all the help she could get. One of Mom's first purchases was a washing machine. Before this time, she had used a washboard to wash the clothes. I have only hazy memories of her doing that, but I have often felt sorry for her having to do all of that hard labor.

Mom, in her later years, always kept her old washboard on display in her living room, along with some other items from those days. Printed across the top of the board was the brand name and then the following line: "The board will do the work for you." I told my mom one time that I would feel sorry for her no more. All of those years I had been sympathetic about all of the hard work that she had done using that washboard. If I had only known—the board was doing all of the work for her.

Actually, knowing advertisers as I do, I suspect that that line may have been a bit of an overstatement. The truth of the matter was that a person could work herself to death with such a board. Somebody still had to rub the clothes against the board, plus a dozen other things that the board was incapable of doing. When my mom bought that board, I really doubt that she was under any illusion about the board doing all of the work for her.

Many of us, however, are under that illusion. We keep looking for some easier, pain-free way of doing things. I am always amazed at the number of pain-free methods that are offered to lose weight. One man said, "I joined a health club last year. I spent about 500 bucks and haven't lost a pound. Apparently, you have to go to the thing."

We also have an innate longing for some pain-free, discipline-free way of living the Christian life. We would like a quick and easy 12-step program for becoming a dynamic Christian without paying the price. Many plans are on the market for just such a Christianity. I have my doubts. As I understand the Bible, there is no short-cut to dynamic discipleship. Jesus said, "If any man will come after me, let him deny himself, take up his cross daily, and follow me." Such a pathway involves long-term discipline and dedication. That kind of discipline is seen in such things as prayer, Bible study, stewardship, and church attendance. We would like a Christian lifestyle where Christ would do all of the work for us. He refuses to offer us such a discipleship.

What Determines Our Message?

There was once a television commercial that showed a preacher preaching to his congregation. He was saying, "Life is like a football game. Our team has the ball on the 35-yard line. There are only one and a half minutes left in the game, and our team has no timeouts because (and he added this with a trace of bitterness in his voice) our coach has stupidly used them up."

About this time the camera angle shifted to a view from behind the preacher showing the congregation out in front. What this angle revealed was that the preacher had a radio earbud in his ear and was evidently listening to the broadcast of the game as he preached. Suddenly his voice rose to a shout, "And we score, we score!" By this time all of the members of the congregation were looking strangely at their pastor who was delivering such a message.

The commercial raised the issue of precisely what determines the message we proclaim. Is it defined by what we hear on the radio or television? Do we echo the latest thing that we have heard? Is the message determined by our culture? The church faces a tricky dilemma here. In an effort to communicate with the modern world, how far do we go in allowing a changing world to shape the method and content of a changeless gospel?

Martin Marty wrote about the trend to allow the market to determine the content and style of our worship. He said, "All serious church bodies are concerned that their traditional forms of worship may not reach a generation whose sensibilities are shaped by supermarkets and television where the attention span of a gnat is too long to use as a measure, immediate sensation is needed, and aesthetic mediocrity is demanded. To do nothing to adapt means stultification and, we are told, dwindling congregations." Then Marty added this note of warning: "To give the whole store away to match what this year's market says the unchurched want is to have the people who know the least about the faith determine most about its expression."

What are we to do—keep an earplug in our ear so that we can proclaim the latest thing that is being said? Allow the world to determine the method and the message? I think not. We need to find a happy medium. Ernest

Campbell observed, "There is a difference between being in touch with the times and being in tune with the times." Ultimately, our message does need to be determined by a voice outside ourselves. It is the still, small voice of God!

The One Who Responds to Your Call

While I was pastor of First Baptist Church in Booneville, Mississippi, we installed an elevator in the church to help people who found it difficult to climb the stairs. Shortly after our elevator was installed, I was sitting in my office one Sunday morning studying my sermon during Sunday School. Deeply immersed in my message, I was jarred back to reality by the ringing of the telephone. I grabbed the receiver and responded, "First Baptist Church, this is Lynn Jones, may I help you?" The voice on the other end of the line said, "This is the 911 office. Do you have an elevator in your church?" I told the emergency officer that we did. He responded, "Well, we just got a call from your elevator."

My first thought was, "Oh, no. We never should have hooked that phone up to the emergency office because the kids will be playing with it all the time and causing false alarms." To cover my embarrassment, I said, "I am so sorry about this. Some of our kids have been riding that elevator, and I am sure that one of them made the call. Please excuse us."

The man on the other end of the line said, "Well, the person who called said that his name is James Chase."

"James Chase?" I said. "Well, that's different. He's our Sunday School Director. I'll check on it, and if we need your help, we'll call back."

I went running over to the elevator, and James had already been rescued. He had not only used the phone in the elevator; he had also been ringing the emergency bell. A couple of people had heard the bell and had used the elevator key to effect the rescue. I apologized to James for trying to brush off the emergency operator. He said that was okay. He added, "You should have heard me trying to convince the 911 operator that First Baptist Church actually had an elevator."

I have often thought of my response that Sunday morning. Here our Sunday School Director was calling for help, and I was turning a deaf ear—trying to dismiss the whole thing.

That is one of our problems in life. Madeliene L'Engle said that we were meant to be finely-turned receivers, but we have created our own static. Messages are no longer clear to us. We lose our ability to tune in.

I'm grateful that God is not like that. He is attentive to the cries of His children. Sometimes we forget that. One little boy wrote a letter to God. In the letter, he asked, "Dear God: Since you retired 2,000 years ago, what kinds of things do you do?"

Well, the fact of the matter is that He has not retired. He has not withdrawn from earth. He is active and involved in the needs of His people.

In his book, Remember, I Love You, Charlie Shedd wrote a beautiful tribute to his wife, Martha. He marveled at her effectiveness in prayer. He said, "I always thought that God must have told His secretary, 'If it's a call from Martha, I'll take it.'"

The good news is that he will also take your call. He will never leave you stranded. You can call on Him today!

Doing the Word

When our son Blake was small, he attended a basketball camp that was being held at our church gym under the direction of a local high school coach. During the week, the coach asked Blake, "Isn't your father a minister?" He said, "No, he's a preacher."

I've thought about that a good bit over the years as I have considered my role. I don't mind being called a preacher because that is at the heart of what I do. When I made a decision to enter the ministry everyone around home said, "He has surrendered to preach." Preaching was seen as the primary activity to which I had committed myself.

I think that's biblical. Paul told Timothy to "preach the Word." I have always enjoyed studying the Word and preaching the Word. "Preacher" is a title that I bear gladly.

But, the title "minister" appeals to me as well. If "preacher" is a word primarily associated with talking about the gospel, "minister" is a word primarily associated with living the gospel. It describes the position as one involving ministry to people who need it.

The highest compliment that one can pay an orator is "well said." The highest compliment that you can pay a philosopher is "well thought." But the highest compliment that you can pay a Christian is "well done." That is the compliment that Jesus paid the faithful steward in Matthew 25. Upon examining his faithful stewardship, Jesus said, "Well done, good and faithful servant!"

The challenge of the Christian life is to go beyond merely talking about the Word of God to doing the Word of God. Over the years, Southern Baptists have often had great debates over the nature of the Word of God. Much of that debate centered around whether you should use the word "inerrant" in connection with the Bible. Tony Campolo spoke to the Southern Baptist Convention during this time of debate. He began with a line that got everyone's attention. He said, "I don't know why you're worrying so much about the inerrancy of the Scripture. After you prove that it's inerrant, you're not going to do what it says anyway."

I would not say that the issue of the inerrancy of Scripture is an unimportant one, but I would agree that an even more critical issue is the matter of doing what the Scripture says. James said that we ought to be doers of the

Word and not hearers only. To be hearers only is to deceive ourselves into thinking that we have done all that is necessary. William Ward said that committing Scripture to memory is admirable; committing it to life is wisdom.

One man said that he was going to join a particular church because he wanted to be fed. That's a good starting place, but it cannot end there. What we need to do frequently is take off the feeding bib and put on the apron of service.

Dealing with Our Basic Problem

I was watching one of those end-of-the-year shows one December. This particular show was reviewing news "bloopers" which had occurred during the year. In one clip there had evidently been a controversy in England over a stretch of the highway on which numerous accidents had occurred. Some people thought this whole section of the road ought to be reconstructed while others opposed the reconstruction project. They insisted that nothing was wrong with this section of the road.

An opponent of the reconstruction project was being interviewed on a TV news program. He was standing near the part of the highway in question with the cars whizzing by in the background. Just as he was emphasizing how safe this section of the road was, a car in the background suddenly left the road and crashed not far behind the man. This scene somehow weakened his case.

Some may insist that sin is not a problem in our day, but the events that surround us point to the seriousness of the situation. Lives are being wrecked and ruined. We must confess our problem. Once we have faced up to the problem, then we have to decide how to deal with it. Too often we take a superficial approach.

When I was pastor of First Baptist Church in Booneville, Mississippi, Vance Brown was a member of our church. Vance began his teaching career by serving as basketball coach at Ashland High School in Northeast Mississippi. One of their most heated rivalries was with a school located nearby, Falkner High School. Vance said that one year they went to Falkner to play, and it was a tight ball game. The lead went back and forth before finally swinging in Ashland's favor. Ashland won by a slim margin. When the game was over, many of the Falkner fans were upset by the outcome of the game. One man was so upset that he pulled a pistol out of his pocket and shot the scoreboard. Police pounced on the man and, fortunately, no one was hurt.

I have often thought of Vance's story because that is the way we sometimes choose to deal with our problems. We fire shots at the scoreboard in the belief that it will somehow change the score. Of course, pumping the scoreboard full of holes does not change the outcome of the game.

In dealing with the problem of our sin, we must get beneath the surface. We must face up to the reality of our sin and come before the Lord with genuine repentance and confession.

One of the ways that Rome dealt with the problems of that great city was to give the people "bread and circuses." That old option would find a place in modern history, but bread and circuses do not deal with the real problems in society or in our lives. Repentance, confession, and forgiveness do. May God help us to get to the root of our problem!

Disclaimer Discipleship

Beware of the dread disclaimer. The disclaimer is the "catch" to all of those wonderful offers that are made to you. Disclaimers are often printed in such small print that only a magnifying glass will enable you to decipher them. For instance, at the bottom of the letter offering you a million dollars is the sentence, "Valid only when redeemed by a person at least 85 years old who is accompanied by both parents."

Or, on radio and television, the disclaimer is given orally. The disclaimer is generally provided in a low voice by the world's fast-talk champion as the music builds to a crescendo. The effect of the disclaimer is mostly to negate the offer that has just been made. The purpose of the ad is to give the impression that something great is being offered while, in reality, nothing of significance is being given. Or, while telling of all of the life-threatening possibilities when taking a drug being advertised, the commercial shows young, healthy people doing things that display their excellent health.

Sometimes disclaimers have a way of sneaking into our religious commitments. Jesus once invited a man to follow Him. The man responded, "Lord, I have always wanted to follow you. You're the most important One in life to me. I will leave all that I have and follow you. But, first, let me go bury my father."

Judging from Jesus' response, the man was evidently tacking on a disclaimer to his commitment. What the man probably meant was that he would follow Jesus after his father died and after he had had an opportunity to bury him. His father likely was in perfect health and would live for many years.

At the end of our pledges of commitment, we often tack on discreet disclaimers. "I will follow you wherever you lead me [within my neighborhood]." "I will do anything that you want me to do [as long as no real effort is required]."

Jesus can spot a disclaimer a mile away. He never has been tolerant of them. To the man who came to Him that day with a "disclaimer-discipleship," Jesus said, "Let the dead bury their dead: but go thou and preach the kingdom of God (Luke 9:60)."

What kind of commitments have you made to Jesus Christ? We need to make unreserved commitments without a single disclaimer.

Expanding Our Circles of Concern

When I was pastor of First Baptist Church of Booneville, Mississippi, one year our Vacation Bible School had an Indiana-Jones-kind-of-theme. Our children were "Truth Trackers" who were tracking down the truth of God's Word. In an effort to reinforce this kind of exotic theme, we challenged the children to give their offerings to buy a llama for the children of Bolivia. We explained how essential llamas are for the people of Bolivia. They produce wool, meat, milk, and serve as beasts of burden. Each llama costs $150.

Our children were very interested in raising money for this project. They went home and told their parents about what we were trying to do and prodded them for money. One little visitor was excited about the project to buy a llama for the children of Bolivia. He went home to tell his parents about it. He said, "And we are trying to raise enough money to buy a llama for the people in Saltillo (a town about 20 miles from Booneville)." The parents were unsure why the people in Saltillo needed a llama, but they were willing to give anyway.

In working with children, you are always trying to expand the horizons of their worlds. You are trying to make them aware of the fact that there are concerns far beyond their own small worlds. I heard of a family that lived in a high-rise apartment building. Each morning as the father would leave for work, his wife and small son would walk down the hallway with him to the elevator and see him off for the day. In the evening, the process would be reversed. The young boy would wait at the elevator with his mother to greet his dad at the end of the workday. One day someone asked the little boy what his dad did for a living. He said, "I don't know, but he spends the whole day on the elevator."

Actually, the elevator was but a means of transit to a broader world. Beyond the narrow walls and sliding doors of this elevator, there was another world of reality. Sometimes our worlds get too small. We lose sight of the fact that there are other matters of great importance beyond the constrictive walls of our familiar worlds.

God's concerns reach around the world. He is as concerned about the people in Bolivia as He is about the people in Saltillo. "God so loved the world that He sent His only begotten son." When our circles of concern become as wide as the circles of God's concern, then we have learned an invaluable lesson about the Christian life and walking in fellowship with the Father.

We had an excellent Vacation Bible School. We bought three llamas for the people of Bolivia. At last report, the people of Saltillo still have no llamas.

Giving People What They Need

Neil Postman, in his book Amusing Ourselves to Death, said that the American story can be defined by four cities which are representative of four periods of our history. Boston represented revolutionary America. It was the center of the independent spirit, which culminated in the creation of a new nation.

New York represented immigrant America. Through that great port city, America welcomed a vast throng of people who came to infuse our land with energy and vision.

Chicago represented industrial America. The move from agricultural to industrial America transformed every aspect of our society.

Today's metaphor city is Las Vegas. The symbols of this culture are a thirty-foot, cardboard cutout of a slot machine and a chorus girl. This city, one of the fastest growing in the United States, is a shrine to the American hunger for amusement. As Postman's title declares, we are "amusing ourselves to death."

This obsession for entertainment and amusement says something about the American way of life. It points to a hunger that we have for something more in life. It declares boredom with the pursuits that occupy much of our time. It enshrines our obsession with escapism. It declares our inattentiveness to ultimate things.

Calvin Miller points out that this hunger on the part of the American people for entertainment impacts the way we do business as a church. The question is, does the church get caught up in an entertainment culture?

Matthew 4 records Jesus' temptation experience. In the second temptation, the Devil took Jesus up upon a high point of the Temple and said, "If you are the Son of God, why don't you just throw yourself down. For it is written, 'He will command his angels concerning you, and they will lift you up in their hands and not a bone of your body will be broken.'"

Here was Satan's invitation to take the show-biz route to messiahship. Talk about an entertaining spectacle—"Man jumps off the pinnacle of the Temple!" People would come from miles around to see a feat like this.

But, upon hearing the offer, Jesus declined. He had not come to put on a good show. He was not interested in amusing the people. He was far more interested in showing them God's love and compassion and in calling them to commitment and dedication.

The church is always walking the fine line between doing things that will attract people and doing things that are true to the God who has called us to represent Him in the world. We are always trying to find the right position between providing things that people want and providing things that they need.

Las Vegas will not be a metaphor city forever. Culture changes. The gospel does not. Instead of amusing people to death, our deepest commitment is to present a gospel that will provide people life.

The Coon in the Sack

It's been said that there are three ways to get something done: 1) Do it yourself, 2) Hire someone to do it, or 3) Forbid your children to do it. It's strange how that works, isn't it? When something is forbidden, it has a peculiar attraction. Maybe it goes all the way back to our original parents.

When God put Adam and Eve in the Garden of Eden, He told them not to eat of the fruit of the tree of the knowledge of good and evil. You know the story. They were convinced, with the serpent's urging, that the Father was keeping something good away from them—something that would enrich their lives. They could not rest until they had sampled the fruit. Mark Twain once suggested that God's mistake was in forbidding Adam and

Eve from eating the fruit of the tree. Instead, Twain said, "God should have put the serpent off limits to them, and they would have eaten it."

We all have this tendency to do what the Father forbids. When I was small, my father was a dedicated coon hunter. When Fibber and Molly were pups, Daddy was very interested in teaching them to trail and tree a coon. So, one evening when he came in from work, he announced that he had gotten a coon from Markell Snell, who was a trapper, and that he had the coon in a sack in his truck. He added, just in passing, that we were not to fool with the coon.

Now, a coon in a sack is an irresistible attraction for a boy, regardless of his father's warning. So, as soon as the coast was clear, I went out to the truck to see the coon. The problem was that the sack was made of burlap and you could not see the coon. All that you could see was what looked like a giant lump at the end of the sack. How could I be sure that there was even a coon in the sack? If it was a coon, was it alive or dead? The longer I thought about it, the greater the temptation to do some investigating.

I finally decided that the best way to resolve the matter was to poke the lump with my finger. So, I sneaked up to the sack and gave the lump a good, stiff poke. When I did, the tow sack exploded. The coon was more alive than I had reckoned. He turned and bit me on the finger. Then the sack jumped about a foot off the ground before tumbling out of the truck and onto the ground.

I thought my finger had been amputated. I screamed at the sight of blood and the growls from inside the sack. My parents came running, and, fortunately, my mom's sympathy for my wound helped cancel out my daddy's anger over my disobeying his instructions to stay away from the coon.

Mark Twain said that if you try to carry a cat home by the tail, you will learn some things you just don't get in a book. I would say the same about poking a coon in a sack.

Doing what the Father says has always been hard on us. But in the long run, we save ourselves a lot of grief by being obedient to His instructions.

Dealing with Our Old Sins

When I was growing up in the country, there were limited forms of entertainment and diversion. In order to fill this gap, the youth of the day devised their own methods of entertainment. In the summer, this often took the form of swiping watermelons from the neighbors.

For some reason, most people saw swiping watermelons as a rather harmless diversion. It was like rolling yards. It was technically forbidden but was tolerated as the price of having young people in the community. In fact, most of the farmers in the area planted a few more melons to cover their losses and turned their heads when they suspected that something might be going on in their fields.

The only time that I ever swiped a watermelon was under the tutelage of my older brother Wayne and his friend Gene Cabra. Under cover of darkness, we sneaked into Norman Herrington's field and got a nice melon. We drove to a secluded spot and ate it. Watermelons eaten under these conditions were always the sweetest and the best.

Several years went by, and I surrendered to preach. When I was 20 years old, I became pastor of Pine Grove Baptist Church where Norman Herrington was a deacon. One Sunday I was visiting with Norman and his wife, Beechel. As we sat around after a big Sunday dinner, I told him that I had a confession to make. I confessed that several years before I had sneaked into his field and had stolen a watermelon. He said that he had always wondered who got that big watermelon that night and was glad to know that it was his future pastor.

A couple of years later we had a revival in our church. The evangelist preached one night on straightening up the sin in our lives. He illustrated the point by telling about an incident in the life of one of his church members. A few weeks before, a man had stopped by to see the member. The man said that when he was a boy, he had stolen a watermelon from the church member. In recent days he had become a Christian and felt convicted of his sin. He then pulled some money out of his pocket and paid the man for the watermelon that he had stolen years before.

I was hoping that Norman Herrington was not in church that night, but I was out of luck. Not only was he at church, but he was waiting for me when the service was over. He said, "Lynn, I heard that story tonight. I'll be waiting for you to stop by and see me."

In a Peanuts comic strip, Lucy once told Charlie Brown, "Sooner or later, you always reap what you sow."

Charlie said, "I'd kind of like to see a little more margin for error."

That's the way with life. Our old sins have a way of coming back to haunt us. There is a price to be paid. I really should have gone by to see Norman about that watermelon, but actually, I figured that I only owed him one-third of its price and that I'd never get Wayne or Gene to pay their fair share.

First-Hand Religion

A young man knocked on the door of a monastery with a large duck in his arms. His uncle, who happened to be one of the monks in the monastery, answered the knock. The nephew said to his uncle, "Here, Uncle, this is a gift for you and the others. Eat it in good health."

The uncle was very grateful. That night the duck was dressed and stuffed. The uncle and the other monks enjoyed a wonderful meal.

A few days later another knock came on the monastery door. The monk opened the door, and the man at the door said, "I am a friend of the nephew who brought you the duck. I have been a bit down on my luck lately, and I wonder if I might impose on you for a bite to eat and a place to sleep for the night?"

The monk replied, "Of course, my son, you are most welcome." And that night, he joined the monks for some warm duck soup.

A few days later, another knock on the door. "Hi, I am a friend of the friend of the nephew who brought the duck. Could I impose on you for a bit of hospitality?" He too was welcomed . . . more duck soup. Several days more went by. Another knock. "Hello, I am a friend of the friend of the friend of the nephew who brought the duck."

That night at dinner he was presented with a steaming hot bowl of water. He tasted it, looked up, and asked, "What's this?" The monk replied, "Well, this is the soup of the soup of the soup of the duck that my nephew brought."

Most of us are not satisfied with fourth-hand soup. Neither should we be satisfied with fourth, third, or even second-hand religion. Our Christianity needs to have the unmistakable marks of a personal encounter about it. Too often it is more distant than that.

Bob Benson once emphasized that point by pointing to the fact that too many artists paint someone else's picture. He said, "We are not willing to take our palette and our paints and our brush and go to the mountains or the forest or the sea and labor until we have captured their beauty on our canvas. We only see their majesty through someone else's eyes and with the strokes of their brush."

Amos gave this account of first-hand religion: "I was neither a prophet nor a prophet's son, but I was a shepherd, and I also took care of sycamore-fig trees. But the Lord took me from tending the flock and said, to me, 'Go, prophesy to my people Israel.' Now then, hear the word of the Lord" (Amos 7:14-16).

Paul bore witness to his own encounter with God: "When God . . . was pleased to reveal his Son in me so that I might preach him among the Gentiles, I did not consult any man" (Gal. 1:15-16).

I thank God for all that we can learn of Him through others. We cannot stop there, however. We must have our own encounters with God. Second-hand experiences always lead to second-rate results. I challenge you to have first-hand experiences with God this week!

The Good News Diet

The subject of numerous books, television shows, and endless conversation is the matter of diets and controlling our weight. Anytime something occupies that much of our time and interest, it is a sure sign that we have a problem on our hands. Controlling our weight in a culture that has more food than we know what to do with is a problem. Someone has said, "Success may go to your head, but it usually makes a rest stop at your waistline."

We struggle with bringing the problem under control. Bill Thorn said of his struggle, "I diet, jog, eat grass, and still have the body of a water buffalo." We're sympathetic. Dieting is a difficult business. That difficulty, however, does not deter those who keep coming up with new and improved diets. Here are a few that you may have missed:

--The balanced diet. This consists of having a Big Mac in both hands.

--The small plate diet. The only problem with this diet is that a lot of your food falls off your plate.

--The light diet. On this diet, one begins eating as soon as it gets light outside.

--The Noah diet. On this diet, you take two of everything.

--The good news diet. Under this plan, you only eat when you hear some good news.

It's this last diet that is of special interest. If you were on the good news diet, how often would you eat? How much weight would you lose? We suffer from a famine in our land. It is a famine of good news.

It is interesting that the word "gospel" meant "good news" in the original language. When casting about for a word to describe the message of Christ's birth, life, death, and resurrection, the early church chose the word meaning "good news."

In a world that is filled with difficulties, we sometimes want to join in the conversation by majoring on bad news. Christians are not escape artists. We do not go around with our heads in the sand insisting that there is nothing bad going on in our world. Probably no one is more aware of the problems in our world than Christians who care. We hurt with every story about sin that destroys people and impoverishes the lives of the survivors. We do not walk around with toothpaste smiles that deny the pain in the lives of our brothers and sisters. A good bit of our time is spent in "weeping with those that weep." But even in the midst of the bad news, we insist that there is good news. Regardless of what is going on, that good news doesn't change!

To Serve and Protect

"To Serve and Protect"—Every time I see that sign on the side of a police car I think of Bro. Walter Barnard. Bro. Walter served for many years as a pastor of Louisiana churches. The final years of his ministry were spent as a Director of Missions in the northeastern part of Louisiana. After retiring, Bro. Walter came back to Springhill, Louisiana, where he had been reared. It was there that I got to know him when I came to be his pastor at Central Baptist Church.

One of the things I always admired about Bro. Walter was his enthusiasm. Most ministers begin their journey from the city of Enthusiasm, but some complete the trip wandering on the road halfway between Depression and Cynicism. Not Bro. Walter. He was always enthusiastic.

Until his dying day, he was convinced that sweeping re-vival, renewal, and rampant church growth were about to begin at any moment. You can't help but admire a man like that.

Bro. Walter, perhaps because of his long experience as a pastor and director of missions, enjoyed enlisting and organizing people. After his retirement, one of his major projects was to organize and promote a soul-winning ral-ly each year at the local Baptist Encampment. One year he suffered a back injury in the weeks leading up to the rally and was hospitalized for several days. His hospital room became a command post. Giving instructions over the telephone, at one time he had all three of our church staff members and both secretaries busy on some of his projects.

He later told me about running into a snag one night when the church office was closed. He was sick of that hospital food and got to thinking about those crispy chick-en-fried steaks over at The Axe restaurant. He called in an order for a big chicken-fried steak but then discovered that they did not deliver. How was he to get the steak to the hospital with the church office closed?

He said, "That's when I remembered that sign on our city police cars—'To Serve and Protect.' I got on the phone to the police station and told them that I needed one of their boys to deliver my chicken-fried steak to the hospi-tal." With a hurt tone in his voice, Bro. Walter said, "Do you know that that fellow on duty down there got a little huffy with me? Why it took a call by me to the Chief at his home before they would bring my chicken-fried steak to the hospital!"

Service is a noble ideal in life. It looks good when plastered across the doors of our automobiles. Actually doing the serving is a good bit more difficult, but it is the thing that is desperately needed. Jesus said, "He that is greatest among you let him be as the younger; and he that is chief, as he that doth serve" (Lk. 22:26). Be careful about the kind of sign you put over your life. You never can tell when someone will come along and take you up on it.

What I Learned from Mr. Prewitt

I don't remember much that Mr. Henry Lee Prewitt taught us in the fifth grade, but I do remember one thing. He wrote on the chalkboard in big letters (and let it stay there for an inordinately long time) this statement: "An excuse only satisfies the person who makes it."

I do not recall what moved Mr. Prewitt to take this side road into the field of philosophy, but I have a hunch. I think it must have been some of the lame excuses that my classmates were making about not having their work done (I feel sure that I was not one of those).

As one person misquoted the Scripture, "An excuse is a very present help in the time of trouble." The Bible is replete with stories of excuses offered by people in trouble. They included the likes of Adam, Eve, Moses, Gideon,

Saul, and some people in a story told by Jesus who had been invited to a great supper.

Mr. Prewitt said, "An excuse only satisfies the person who makes it." I must add, however, that some excuses also bring a smile to others. Consider the following:

--A man asked his boss if he could have the day off. His boss said, "I suppose it's for your grandfather's funeral. You've already been off four times for his funeral. Is that why you want off?"

The man responded, "No, sir. I'd like to get off because my grandmother is getting remarried."

--When the old cat let out a yowl in the den, the mother shouted to her four-year-old, "Are you pulling the cat's tail?"

The four-year-old replied, "No. I'm just holding her tail. She's doing all of the pulling."

--A man was before the judge on the charge of stealing a car. The judge asked, "Why did you take the car?"

The man said, "The car was parked next to the cemetery, and I assumed that the owner was dead."

I don't know if you have ever offered such excuses, but if all the excuses that we have given were written down, most of them would look pretty lame—especially the excuses we have offered God.

God has been hearing excuses ever since Adam and Eve offered theirs, and He can see through all of them. He challenges us to be honest and responsible for our lives. But it's hard for us to assume responsibility.

Did you hear about the golfer who went to the first hole with his caddy? Just as he was about to hit his drive, the caddy hiccupped. The man hit a terrible drive and blamed the caddy for disrupting his concentration. This continued throughout the round. The caddy continued to hiccup at critical times, and the golfer continued to have a terrible round. When they arrived at the 18th hole, the golfer drove off the tee into a water hazard. When that happened, he exploded on the caddy. The caddy said, "But sir, I didn't hiccup that time." The man said, "That's just the point. I was compensating for it."

Got any old excuses that you need to discard? Remember, as Mr. Henry Lee Prewitt wrote on the chalkboard, "An excuse only satisfies the person who makes it."

Lasting Impacts

One of the most meaningful things about teaching is the opportunity to make an impact on the lives of students at a young and impressionable age. Fifty years ago, when I was 21, in addition to becoming pastor of Pine Grove Baptist Church in Peason, Louisiana, I began teaching English and social studies at Florien High School in Florien, Louisiana. Two students that I taught were Dale Ellzey and Mary Jordan. After they graduated from high school, they were married and had four children.

Dale became a Marine Corps helicopter pilot. In 1986, while flying off the coast of Norway, his helicopter went down, and he was killed. Two years ago his wife Mary wrote on Facebook about that awful day when she learned of his death and the days that followed. When I read her post only recently, I wrote a response to her article, and then she replied to my comments. Here is what

I wrote a few days ago, and this is what Mary wrote this morning:

Lynn: "It was my privilege to teach Dale and Mary at Florien High School when we were all young and the world lay out before us with all its possibilities. I had known Dale's family all of my life, growing up across the field from them at Plainview. I got to know Dale better as we plowed through freshman and sophomore English together. He was a great student. He worked hard, always did his best to do what was assigned, and was a joy to be around. I moved on from teaching to the ministry, but kept up with him, Mary, and their children from afar. I was touched by news of his death. May God bless all of us as we remember and thank God for the gift of Dale's life that blessed and enriched us all!"

Mary: "Mr. Jones, we both thought so much of you as a teacher. One of the best things that you did for us was to assign the paper on the life of someone close to us. Dale wrote about his grandmother Ellzey (interviewing her). I wrote about my grandmother Jordan (interviewing my Aunt Josie, who was the family keeper of the stories). I still have both [papers], originals, in our handwriting and pages tied together with yarn. Precious to me. Thank you for your willingness to teach us."

This is the first correspondence that Mary and I had had between us in almost fifty years. I sit here this morning in Oxford remembering these two fine young people that I taught. At the time I taught them, I had no idea that they would get married or that Dale would go half-a-world away to be killed in a helicopter crash in the service of his country. I had no idea that fifty years after I gave them that assignment, to write the story of the life of someone close to them, that Mary would still have the papers that they turned in and holds onto them as something precious.

Since this exchange, Mary died of cancer. I will always remember her bravery and faith in facing that. Today I remember and give thanks to God that I had the opportunity to make a small contribution to the lives of these two wonderful people. Be careful today. You never know when something you are teaching, preaching, saying, or doing will make a lasting impact on someone's life!

The Lure of Larceny

I read of a car that was burglarized. The only thing taken was the car alarm. Perhaps it is a sign of the times.

A reporter decided to survey people on their opinion about crime. He walked the streets and asked over 50 people if they thought there was too much crime on the streets. Sixty-two percent of those surveyed said "yes." Twenty-three percent said "no." The other 15 percent tried to mug the guy taking the survey.

We are concerned and critical of those on the street who steal. It has been my experience, however, that sometimes stealing takes place much closer to home. Sometimes it even takes place at church.

In one church of which I was pastor, we had to retrieve from a pawn shop some items that had been stolen from the church by a custodian. In another church, an offering had been taken for a visiting musical group. After the offering was collected, the plate was not watched carefully, and somebody helped himself to the entire offering.

In one church where I served, somebody even stole my Bible. They kept it for five years before their conscience evidently started bothering them. They mailed it back to me in a plain brown envelope. It didn't look like it had been used much in its absence.

When I served as pastor of First Baptist Church in Newark, Texas, several churches in the area were robbed during their worship services. A gang of men actually came into the sanctuaries as worship was going on, held guns on the worshipers, and took their money and jewelry.

During that time, we were always a little nervous when we met for worship. One Sunday night about ten minutes after the service had begun, one of our worshipers entered the door at the back and gave it a big rattle as he closed it. Everybody in the congregation jumped, including me. Fortunately, the robbers were arrested a few weeks later, and everybody began to relax a bit.

With robbery so rampant, many do not take it as seriously as they ought. In fact, all of us may be guilty of a little larceny on occasion. Consider the matter of work. We agree to do a certain amount of work for a specific wage. If we do not work as promised, are we guilty of a form of robbery? Or, you take the matter of paying taxes. Some people feel entirely justified in cheating on their taxes. As long as the crime is committed against a big, faceless agency like the IRS, they see it as different. Is it?

Or, you take the matter of tithes and offerings. Malachi said that those who were not faithful in bringing their tithes and offering to God were guilty of robbery. That's not the last time that crime has been committed.

A man went to trade cars, and the car salesman offered him only $5,000 for his car. The salesman said, "That's what the Blue Book says it's worth." The man pulled out a Bible and responded, "Here is a black book, and it says 'Thou shalt not steal.'" So it does. And all of us ought to listen to it.

Getting Even with People

One time I did a post on Facebook in which I asked, "When we talk about getting even with someone, why is it that we always talk about getting even with someone who has mistreated us? Why not talk about getting even with the people who have helped us?"

Later that day, David Jett made a comment on my post that took me back in time about 35 years. Thirty-five years before I was serving as pastor of First Baptist Church in Arcadia, Louisiana. One night as Danielle and I were asleep in that big parsonage on the side of the hill, there was a knock on our door about 2:00 AM. I have lived long enough to know that people who knock on your door at 2:00 o'clock in the morning have not come to bring you good news.

I jumped out of bed, pulled on some clothes, and opened the door. A young Louisiana State Trooper was standing at my door. I recognized him as David Jett, a friend of mine who had been reared not far from me at Hornbeck, Louisiana.

He said, "Lynn, I hate to disturb you this late at night, but there has been a bad accident on Interstate 20. Billy Atteridge was driving east on I-20 when a drunk driver entered the interstate at the Haughton exit and started driving the wrong way on the highway. The drunk driver headed west on the interstate in the eastbound lanes. After a short distance, the driver had a head-on collision with the car driven by Billy Atteridge, and Billy was killed instantly. I understand that he and his family are members of your church, and I have to go tell his parents about his death. I was wondering if you would go with me to tell them."

I told him that I would. So, I hurriedly got dressed and told him to follow me to the home of Bill and Irene Atteridge. As a preacher, I have had the opportunity to share the good news every Sunday for over 50 years, but every now and then, I have had to share some bad news, and I have never had to share any worse news than I had to share that night. We knocked on the door, and when Bill and Irene saw their pastor and a State Trooper standing at the door, they immediately knew that we had no good news to share with them.

We told them that we needed to talk to them. We went into the living room, sat down, and, in a voice broken by emotion, I told Bill and Irene that their son Billy had been killed in an automobile accident. David gave them more details about how the accident had occurred. Thanks to the temporary anesthetic of shock that God provides in such moments, they were able to withstand the initial jolt of the news. We stayed there for a while, other friends came to offer support, I led them in prayer, and then David and I left. The day of the funeral soon arrived and was over, but for Bill and Irene, the days of mourning were not over. That went on and on and followed them to some degree the rest of their lives.

David is now retired from the State Troopers, and thirty-five years have passed since that awful night, but he has not forgotten it, and neither have I. When I made the post last week about getting even with people who have helped us, David, who is now my friend on Facebook, read it, and made the following comment: "Lynn, you blessed my life one very late night in Arcadia, Louisiana. I may have been able to complete that task without you, but certainly not as well. Try as I might, I will never be able to get even with you for that. Thanks."

I also need to thank David for giving me strength that night to help deliver that message and for the gift of his gratitude that he presented to me last week. I think we're even now.

It's a harsh world out there with many challenges. Let's help each other. And then let's try our best to get even with every person who helps us along the way!

Laying Down Your Life for Your Brother

In the 1950's tonsillectomies were wildly popular with parents of small children. I know because they were popular with my parents. Because my two brothers and I had sporadic problems with our tonsils, my mother had an almost religious fervor about her obligation to have our tonsils removed. When my older brother Wayne continued to have issues with his tonsils, he had them removed in the early 50's. I didn't have as many problems with my tonsils, but my younger brother Rick did. So, my mom arranged for him to have his tonsils removed as well.

When they carried Rick to have his tonsils out, however, they ran into problems. He developed a fever, and they had to postpone the procedure. Later on, they ran into the same problem when they scheduled the surgery again. They concluded that Rick was so frightened by the prospect of surgery that he was developing a fever. So, my mom was in a quandary about what to do. She finally hit upon a new plan, which, unfortunately, involved me. She decided that if I had my tonsils removed at the same time that Rick had his removed it would keep Rick calm and he would not develop a fever.

So, one night she broached the subject to me. She admitted that while my tonsils were not bothering me much, it would be a wonderful thing if I could have them taken out to help my brother. She didn't say this, but I got the impression that I would be like one of those stable horses that comes out onto the track with a thoroughbred before a race to keep him calm. Rick wasn't a thoroughbred, but he was as skittish as a thoroughbred.

My mom quoted the Scripture about our loving our neighbor as much as we loved ourselves, but I didn't see the connection because Rick was my brother, not my neighbor, and he was considerably harder to love than the folks down the road that you didn't have to put up with all the time. But then she moved on from Scripture to talking about how brave I was, how she would buy us some new pajamas when we went into the hospital, and how when my throat was sore after the surgery I could eat all of the ice cream that I wanted. I wasn't swayed by talk about the Scripture or the pajamas, but talk about how brave I was and the thought of eating all the ice cream that I wanted completely won me over, and I agreed to have my tonsils out at the same time Rick did.

So, after agreeing to be a sacrificial lamb to cover my brother's weakness, the big date for our tonsillectomies was set. We went to Fraser's Sanitarium in Many, Louisiana, for the surgery. You will notice that not many hospitals are called "sanitariums" these days. I wasn't sure what that name meant, but I thought it must mean that it was a sanitary place, and you couldn't argue with that when you were going to undergo surgery there.

On the day scheduled for our surgery, my uncle and aunt, Lewis and Fourthie Cole, came to the hospital to join our parents for the surgery. The nurses were preparing us for surgery, and when they checked Rick's temperature, he had the fever. My reassuring presence with him had not made a bit of difference. He was scared to death anyway, and this had evidently caused him to develop the fever. This put my parents in a quandary about whether to go ahead with my surgery since I didn't need it anyway, and I had obviously failed to keep my brother calm. So, they asked me if I wanted to go ahead with it.

If I had had good judgment, I would have jumped at the chance to avoid surgery, but for some strange reason, I didn't. My parents and my aunt and uncle were here. They were bragging on my courage, and the prospect of having all of that ice cream was on my mind, so, I sat up in bed and said, "Sure, I think I want to go ahead with my surgery." I impressed absolutely everyone with my bravery and resolve. It was a wonderful moment. Unfortunately, it was soon over, and I was on my way to surgery.

Today, being put to sleep for surgery takes place before you know what has happened. In those days, they used ether as an anesthetic, and it was not quick, and it was not pleasant at all. It has been 60 years since they used it on me, and I can remember exactly how it felt. I will spare you the details, but it was one of the most unpleasant things I have ever been through in my life. Soon, the surgery was over, and I was sent home the next day. I was terribly uncomfortable for a few days and didn't even feel like eating any ice cream. Not only did I have to put up with the pain and discomfort, but I also had to put up with seeing Rick outside the window frolicking in the yard with our friends and his coming in to eat most of the ice cream that my mom had bought.

Not only was the surgery rough, but also it didn't work. My tonsils grew back over the years. Rick never had his tonsils removed, continued to grow and do well, and became six feet tall while I stalled out at 5' 8". I still have some resentment toward him about this whole tonsillectomy episode, but I'm trying to get over it. One of the things that has helped is that Rick has occasionally expressed some gratitude to me for one of the noblest things that I have ever done.

John said, "We ought to lay down our lives for our brothers" (1 John 3:16). That is a high and holy calling, and

I have a long way to go before I am able to reach that level of maturity and sacrificial love. But at least on a long-ago day when I was very young, I was willing at least to lay down my tonsils for my brother.

Judging a Sermon

When our son Blake was a boy, his motor was always racing, and getting him to go to sleep at night was a challenge. So, often at night, Danielle would give me the chore of getting him to sleep. I would usually think of a good Bible story that I planned on telling him. So, I would turn off the light, lie down beside him, and then it was on—He would hit me over the head with his pillow. What could I do? I had to defend myself, so I would hit him with my pillow. For the next five minutes, the pillow fight would rage back and forth.

Most child-rearing experts will tell you that a big pillow fight is not the best tactic to use to induce sleep in a hyperactive boy. So, finally, after several minutes of this raging battle, I tried to defuse the situation by persuading Blake to listen to a story that I had to tell him. The only problem was that he had grabbed my pillow and would not give it back to me. After threatening him if he didn't give the pillow back, he said, "You tell the story, and if the story is any good I will give your pillow back to you."

Now that is one of the toughest challenges that I've ever faced with a story or a sermon. What if he didn't like the story? Would we be up all night? Would I have to lie beside him until he went to sleep without a pillow under my head? I searched the files of my mind and went for a tried-and-true story that always appeals to boys—the story of David and Goliath. I told it with as much vividness as possible. I embellished the Scripture a little with some added details (A man has to do what he has to do in order to get his pillow back). I emphasized the risk that the boy David was running, his bravery against great odds, and his faith in the face of great danger. I told of every stone that David picked up and of the immensity of Goliath's armor. I gave a blow-by-blow description of the battle. I stretched the story out as long as I could in hopes that Blake would relax a little, get a bit sleepy, and put aside any plans that he had to resume the pillow fight.

I remembered his condition—I wouldn't get my pillow back if the story wasn't any good. I finished with the story with the sound of the "thud" of the giant hitting the ground and the triumphant David being acclaimed as a hero by the army of Israel. Then I waited in the darkness in dead silence. Finally, mercifully, my pillow came flying across the bed, hit me squarely in my face, and Blake rolled over and went to sleep.

It is a very subjective thing to judge how good a sermon or a story is. All kinds of measuring devices have been used. I just know that for me, being awarded a pillow for a message that I delivered one night to a very tough audience is one the single highest compliments that I have ever received for a message I have shared.

Showing Your Faith in a Graveyard

Death was different when I was growing up. The pain and sorrow that it caused were not unusual, but what people did at death was different. We had no funeral homes in Plainview, and, at the time, it was not the custom to carry the body to the church for visitation. Instead, they brought the body home where friends and neighbors came to the home of the person who had died for visitation. Not only that, but funeral homes generally did not handle the preparation of the grave for burial. Instead, my dad would often go with other neighbors to dig the grave at Prewitt's Chapel Cemetery, where most his family and many of our neighbors were buried.

Prewitt's Chapel Cemetery was situated on a hill with concrete masquerading as clay located about one inch

109

beneath the surface. Digging that rock-hard clay in the middle of a dry summer was one final act of love, honor, and respect that my dad and others rendered to some friend who had died. Their sympathy was not expressed in the words they spoke but in their hard work hacking away at the uncompromising clay on that hill that had seen so much sorrow.

When Jesus died, Joseph of Arimathea and Nicodemus did something like that. On this Friday years ago, they did not talk about their love for Jesus, but they acted it out by taking His body, wrapping it in burial clothes, anointing it with myrrh and aloes, and placing it in a grave. They acted out their sorrow, expressed their love, and prepared the place where the world's greatest miracle, the resurrection, would take place on Sunday.

My dad's body now lies buried beneath that unforgiving Prewitt's Chapel Cemetery clay that he so often had turned with his shovel during his lifetime. He is now with the Lord, and the final word has not yet been spoken over Prewitt's Chapel Cemetery. That word will be spoken when Christ descends from heaven with a shout, with the voice of the archangel, and with the trumpet of God, and resurrection will come!

Help Wanted

I often see a message posted at area businesses. Sometimes the sign is in the window or on the door. Sometimes it is displayed in big letters on an outdoor display board. The sign reads: HELP WANTED. What the sign indicates is that the business is short-handed. It has more work than it can currently handle.

It would be good, I think, to get some of those signs and pass them around to all of the people that we could. Then, when people need some help, they could hang out that sign and others could respond.

One of the reasons that such a sign would be helpful is because sooner or later everyone needs a little help. Sometimes the need is for someone to come alongside and lend a listening ear. Sometimes it is a need for someone to help in other ways.

Of course, even if we distributed such signs, there is no guarantee that persons would use them. One of the earliest lines that we learned as we tried to establish our independence was, "I can do it by myself." To admit there are some things we cannot do by ourselves is often very threatening. We resist such an admission at all cost. Our "HELP WANTED" signs languish in the corner gathering dust.

The New Testament never fosters the notion that all of us ought to be self-sufficient, not needing anyone's help. Paul advised the Christians in Galatia to "Bear one another's burdens and so fulfill the law of Christ" (Gal. 6:2). The verse suggests that we all have burdens and that we ought to take turns helping each other out as we bear them.

Since most people are reluctant to hang out HELP WANTED signs, we have to be especially sensitive in order to find those who need help.

In Greek mythology, there is the story of Narcissus. Narcissus saw his image mirrored in a pool of water and was captivated by it. He could not attend to any of his needs other than the need to admire and love himself in the mirrored pool. As a result, he soon died. The "narcissus complex" in which we are enamored with ourselves makes us blind to the need for help in the lives of others.

What we need to do is cultivate sympathy and sensitivity in the rich, organic soil of love for others. Carlyle Marney once said, "I go carefully around corners because

I never know when I will run smack into Christ in someone who is hurting."

As you go around this week, keep your eyes peeled for people who need a little help, even if they do not have a HELP WANTED sign posted. One other thing—if you are struggling with bearing your own burden, don't be afraid to post the HELP WANTED sign in the window of your own life.

Religion for the Road

On Tuesday, January 22, 1985, Judge Frank Eppes walked into county court in Aiken, South Carolina. Judge Eppes' custom was to call on someone to lead in prayer to open the session. On this day he asked if there was a minister present in the courtroom who would open the session with prayer. Rev. Gilbert Gooden of Andrews, South Carolina, was present. He stood and led in prayer.

It was not until later in the session that it became apparent why Bro. Gooden was present in court that day. He was there to face charges of resisting arrest after his car was clocked doing 91 miles-per-hour on the interstate. After learning of this, the judge released Gooden and told him to come back to the court's next term. Although

I never read, I assume that he was not asked to lead in prayer at the later term.

Now, whatever else you think of Gooden, you'll have to admit one thing—the man has a lot of nerve. For myself, there are times when I had just as soon not have folks know that I'm a preacher. Right after receiving a speeding ticket is one such moment. One of my most embarrassing experiences came while I was pastor of First Baptist Church of Newark, Texas. Our choir had just sung at an associational choir festival in Bridgeport, Texas. Danielle and I left in our car shortly before the rest of the choir. We were making excellent time on the way home when a highway patrolman pulled me over to explain that I was making too much time. While he was telling this to me, the entire church choir passed by. What a moment! At least when they yelled at me, they were in perfect harmony.

Making the transition from the pulpit and the pew to the highways of life is difficult isn't it? But, if you will pardon the expression, it is where the rubber meets the road. The important thing is not just how we drive, but also how we talk, how we relate to people where we live, where we play, and where we work. Christianity is not just a weekend job. It is a way of life. God can give us the grace to live it this week so that at any moment we will be unashamed to stand and be identified with Him!

Horizons

I grew up in a country community in West-Central Louisiana called "Plainview." Most people, when they think of Louisiana, think of flat land, swamps, bayous, seafood, and Cajun accents. That's the way it is for folks living in South Louisiana, but we didn't live in South Louisiana. We lived in the northern part of Louisiana. This part of the state was a hilly land with sand beds, pine trees, purple hull peas, and country accents. In most parts of Louisiana, you can't see very far into the distance because of all the trees. But when my ancestors and others came to our community, they could see so far that they called it "Plainview." There is a Plainview in West Texas, but I didn't know anything about that one when I was growing up. I thought our Plainview was the only one in the world.

Plainview School was located on a high ridge that gave you a view of all the country around, especially to the west. Thirty years before I was born, my ancestors and others, with a remarkable lack of vision or environmental concern, joined forces with big timber and land companies to cut all of the virgin pine forests in that part of the state. My grandfathers and others found work related to the timber industries, but it was short-lived. The timber companies followed the policy of "cut out and get out."

They cut every tree, leaving behind a denuded landscape, gullies that washed deep into hillsides, and scraggly bushes behind them. But, there was one bright spot in all of this environmental carnage—they left behind horizons. You could see a long way. Looking out of our elementary school windows to the west, I could see far horizons and dream boyhood dreams of what lay out there in the future for me. Haddon Robinson said, "We all live under the same sky, but we don't all see the same horizon." I am grateful that I grew up in a place where I had a "plain view" of distant horizons and spent a lot of time thinking and dreaming about what lay out there as I made my plans for one day marching over that horizon!

How Fast Are You Going?

There's a story about two city slickers who decided that they had had it with city living. They wanted to get back to the simpler things of life, so they bought a ranch in West Texas. The goal of these two latter-day pioneers was to live off the land like their ancestors. To make this a reality, they decided they needed to buy a mule. They went to a neighboring rancher and asked him if he had a mule to sell. The rancher told them that he did not.

The two city slickers were disappointed, but as they visited with the rancher for a few moments, one of them saw some honeydew melons stacked against the barn and asked, "What are those?" The rancher decided to have some fun with these two novices. "Oh," he answered, "those are mule eggs. You take one of those eggs home and wait for it to hatch, and you'll have a mule."

The city slickers were overjoyed at this, so they bought one of the melons and headed down the bumpy country road toward their own ranch. Suddenly they hit an especially treacherous bump, and the honeydew melon bounced out the back of the pickup truck, hit the road, and burst open. Seeing in his rearview mirror what had happened, the driver turned his truck around and drove back to see if he could retrieve his mule egg.

Meanwhile, a big Texas jackrabbit came hopping by and saw this honeydew melon burst in the road. He hopped over to it and, standing in the middle of the burst melon, he began to eat. Now here came the two city slickers. They spied their mule egg burst open and this long-eared creature in the middle of it. One of the men shouted, "Our mule egg has hatched. Let's get our mule."

But seeing those two men coming toward him, the jackrabbit took off, hopping in every direction with the two city fellows in hot pursuit. The two city slickers gave it everything they had to catch him, but finally, they could go no farther. Both men fell to the ground gasping for air while the jackrabbit hopped off into the distance.

Raising up on his elbow, one of the men said to the other, "Well, I guess we lost our mule."

The other man nodded grimly, "Yes, but you know," he said, "I'm not sure I wanted to plow that fast anyway."

We live in a fast-paced world. In Willa Cather's Death Comes to the Archbishop, Eusibius, a wise old Navajo says, "Men travel faster now, but I do not know if they go to better things." How fast are you going and exactly where is it taking you? This week, slacken your pace for times of fellowship with God.

How to Face the Testing Times

Some folks are eternally optimistic. Others are perpetually pessimistic. Some can spot a ray of hope on the darkest day. Others can detect a small cloud on the sunniest day. I have always admired those who can find the best in difficult situations. Someone has said that you can always spot an optimistic person. He's the guy who sees a housefly buzzing through his living room and thinks that the fly is looking for a way out of the house.

That person may be a figment of someone's imagination, but I read of a person who has a name and an identity. His name is Doug Weaver. He is a former football coach at Kansas State. During his tenure at the school, some students hung him in effigy in front of the university library. When asked what he thought of that, Weaver responded, "I'm glad it happened in front of the library. I've always emphasized scholarship."

Now that's the kind of guy that I admire. He didn't overreact. He didn't let a severe situation overwhelm him. He reminds me of a man who was once put into prison. When that happened to him, he said, "I am so grateful that this imprisonment has given me the opportunity to witness to so many people." When he was stricken with a severe illness, he did not give up. In fact, he said that he was grateful for the illness because it had led him to experience so much of the power of God. When he faced other difficulties, he always rejoiced over them. He said that they produced perseverance, character, and hope.

That man's name was Paul, and the details of those reactions can be examined in Phil. 1:12-14, 2 Cor. 12:7-10, and Rom. 5:1-5. His reaction to those difficulties was not based upon some shallow optimism. It was based on the profound hope and strength, which were his (and ours) in Jesus Christ.

How do you react to such moments? If you are like most people, you do not handle those times very well. One of the things that James advised was this. He said, "Count it all joy when you fall into different testings" (James 1:2). Literally, we are to "consider" it all joy. Commitment to such a reaction must be made before the difficult moment arrives. When the testing time arrives, you will no longer have any time to prepare for it. This must be your premeditated response to such moments. May God help us make that a reality in our lives!

Living with Red Mare

It's humbling growing up with a horse that knows more than you. I know because I did.

She did not have an exciting name (her name was "Red Mare"). She was not especially pretty (as her name implies, she was a "red mare"). She was not very sure of foot (she could stumble on any clod of dirt). And she was not very brave (she would "shy" at a black stump, a wooden bridge, or anything flapping in the wind).

In spite of her obvious shortcomings, she made up for them by several positive qualities. She tolerated pestering by small boys (with a degree of contempt, I might add). And she had a storehouse of wisdom about the ways of the farm (which, unfortunately, she often put to devious use).

Red Mare had spent 15 years or so on the farm before I came along, so she had a head start in absorbing the wisdom of the place. This edge in wisdom allowed her to manipulate small boys.

She had all kinds of manipulative tricks she used to prevent us from riding her. She would hold her head up high to keep us from putting the bridle on. She would grit her teeth so we couldn't put the bit in her mouth. She would stand far away from us when we were trying to throw a heavy saddle on her. She would inhale enormous quantities of air when you tried to tighten the girth so that later she could exhale when you put your foot in the stirrup, and the saddle would slip off her back. If you did jump through all of these hoops and get on her for a ride, you could hardly get her to walk away from the house. If, however, you turned her back toward the house she broke into a run and would run under low-hanging branches if you didn't keep a tight rein on her.

Her most sophisticated repertoire of tricks was used to try to get herself something to eat. She could open almost any gate on the place. A wire hoop over a gatepost she could remove in seconds. A chain slipped over a nail was like an open gate to her. A single latch turned crosswise on a crib door was a posted invitation to dinner.

She kept her eye open for any gate or door that had been left ajar or not closed with two or three latches. Boys generally do not have time to fool with such things as closing gates and doors behind them, but with Red

Mare on the place closing gates securely was a necessity. Our parents drilled that into us constantly.

In fact, I owe to Red Mare one of the most important lessons that I ever learned. It was the importance of closing a gate behind me. That's important, not just on a farm with a pesky horse, but in all of life. All of us have painful things in our past. We cannot undo those things. What we need to do is repent of our sins and receive the forgiveness of God. Then, we need to close the gate behind us. All of us have things we wish we had done differently, but we cannot change those things. We need to close the gate behind us. Paul did that. He said that he was "forgetting those things which are behind and reaching forth unto those things which are before."

How about you? Got any gates that you need to close behind you?

Keeping the Infrastructure Strong

A phrase that I hear a lot these days is "rebuilding our infrastructure." Usually, when the term is used today, it denotes some basic elements in a nation—things like roads, financial systems, distribution systems, power systems, etc. We generally take such aspects for granted until they begin to break down. Then we realize how essential they are for our existence.

While all of the parts of our economic and business infrastructure are important, it seems to me that we also have essential personal infrastructures that are critical for life. Again, we take these pretty much for granted until they are threatened. Then, that is all that we can think of.

One of our needs is to give attention to this infrastructure before it begins to crumble.

Take the matter of our family and personal relationships. Nothing is more essential to our happiness and well-being, but we can neglect these with dire consequences. A study was done to try to determine what healthy families have in common. Here are the findings of the study: 1) Family members are committed to the family; 2) They spend time together; 3) They have good family communication; 4) They express appreciation to each other; 5) They have a spiritual commitment; 6) They are able to solve problems in a crisis. Attention to these matters can shore up our family infrastructure.

Or, take the matter of our spiritual infrastructure—how can we keep it strong? I heard of one woman who boasted that she had gone through the Louvre in one hour. She said that she could have done it in less time if she had not had on high heels. That spirit dominates our spiritual life. Hymn writer W. D. Longstagg gave us a clue to a healthy spiritual life. He wrote, "Take time to be holy." That's what it takes—time. Time to pray, time to read the Bible, time to express gratitude and praise. How much time do you invest in keeping your spiritual infrastructure strong?

Or, take the matter of our church life—how do we maintain our strength? A man noticed some curious behavior by a teenager in his neighborhood. Every day she walked to the mailbox in front of her house and spent about 30 minutes jumping up and down. When he inquired about this, she explained that she was taking a cheerleading course by correspondence. Some people want to do their church work by correspondence. They communicate from a distance and are never personally involved. Without a consistent investment of the best we have, the church infrastructure can begin to crumble.

How much are you investing in your personal infrastructure? Don't wait until it begins to crumble before becoming concerned.

Learning from a Story

Bro. Avon Cavanaugh came to be pastor of First Baptist Church in Florien, Louisiana while I was teaching school there and serving as pastor of Pine Grove Baptist Church in the late 60's. Bro. Cavanaugh became my friend, and ten years later, when I was completing my seminary degrees at Southwestern Seminary and serving as pastor of First Baptist Church, Newark, near Fort Worth, I had Bro. Cavanaugh preach a revival for me at the church. I always loved his preaching and his sense of humor. During the week, we went to the home of Bro. Floyd Norris for a meal. After the lunch, Bro. Cavanaugh and Glen Norris, Floyd's brother who was visiting, began telling stories. Glen was from Arkansas and Bro. Cavanaugh was from

Louisiana, so each of them felt obligated to tell a story about his home state.

Bro. Cavanaugh said that Louisiana was noted for having a lot of poor, crooked roads. He said that there was once a farmer who had a cornfield a couple of miles down the road from his house. When the corn was ready to be pulled, the farmer and his two sons went to the field, pulled the corn, and threw it into piles in the "heap rows." When they were through pulling the corn, they went to the house, hooked their two horses to the wagon, and brought the wagon to the field. They loaded the wagon with as much corn as it would hold and then went down the crooked road to their barn.

When they got to the barn, they discovered that a lot of the corn was missing from the wagon, and they couldn't figure out what had happened to the corn. On their second trip with the loaded wagon, it was the same. So, on the third trip from the field to the barn, they watched the wagon closely and discovered what was happening to the corn. The road between the field and the barn was so crooked and had so many hairpin curves in it that along the way the two horses that were pulling the load were eating most of the corn out of the wagon! Now, that was a crooked road!

Not to be outdone, Glen Norris bragged about how tough Arkansas razorbacks were. He said that a farmer near him was dynamiting stumps on his farm. The farmer put a stick of dynamite under a stump, lit the fuse, and went running away to a safe place where he awaited the blast. Just as he turned to run away, an old razorback hog came running by the stump, grabbed the stick of dynamite with the burning fuse in his mouth, and went running across the field to the barn that stood at the edge of the field. Just as the razorback entered the barn, the stick of dynamite exploded. When asked what kind of damage the explosion had done, the farmer said, "Well, it was sad. The explosion completely destroyed the barn, killed two horses and one cow, and for a couple of days there we had a mighty sick hog."

I enjoyed listening to the stories that Glen and Bro. Cavanaugh told that day, and I learned from them. I learned from Glen's story that if we are going to survive in life, toughness is needed. And, I learned from Bro. Cavanaugh's story that in a world with many crooked roads we need to carry on the ministry of John the Baptist. Matthew said that before Jesus came, John was "A voice of one calling in the desert, 'Prepare the way for the Lord, make straight paths for him'" (Matt. 3:3).

The Seasons of Life

We live in a region of marked seasons. Summer comes with its scorching middays and winter follows with its icy mornings. Dealing with extremes is a challenge.

Some of the members of the animal kingdom are not equipped to deal with such extremes. In order to deal with fluctuations in temperature, they adopt one of two responses. They either migrate, or they hibernate.

Birds are the most famous migratory animals. Typically, from here they head to South America during our winter season and then return when the days begin lengthening and warming. Their ability to maintain their sense of direction is amazing. No one knows precisely how they do it, although most scientists suggest that they plot their courses by the sun and stars or by sensitivity to the earth's magnetic field.

Hibernation is a response adopted by some animals. The woodchuck enters into the deep sleep of hibernation during the cold winter months. During that time its heart may beat only four or five times a minute. Its body temperature drops as low as 37 degrees. It is only with the warming days of spring that its metabolic rate quickens and it emerges from under the anesthetic of hibernation sleep.

How do humans cope with such extreme conditions? While a few migrate to warmer locations in winter and then reverse the move in summer, most folks stay put. And, while we may slacken our outdoor activities during the winter, we do not hibernate. Instead, we find coping mechanisms. We put on thicker clothing and turn up the thermostat. We have an amazing ability to survive in extremes of cold and heat.

We have the same flexibility when it comes to coping with other extreme kinds of pressure. I suppose that all of us have had the desire to escape the pressure of the moment by migrating to some more pleasant place. We have felt like the psalmist who said, "Oh, that I had the wings of a dove! I would fly away and be at rest" (Ps. 55:6). On other occasions, we have felt like Elijah who tried to escape the pressure by going into a cave on Mount Horeb and entering at least a temporary period of hibernation.

What God wants from us, however, is not hibernation or migration. He wants to give us the grace to cope with the extremes that we encounter in the places where we live. He offers us the reassuring words: "My grace is sufficient for thee."

I agree with Edwin Way Teale, who has written about animal migration and hibernation. He concluded, "[My wife and I] desire no migrant's year of one continued summer, no hibernator's year half lost in unconsciousness. We want the whole year, the year rounded with spring and summer and autumn and winter, with the variety of all its seasons." May God bless you in the midst of all the seasons of your life!

Life Is a Gift

I see all of my years of life as a gift from God, but especially the last 50 of those years. Let me tell you why. In the summer of 1966, I had completed my first year at Southwestern Seminary in Fort Worth and had come home that summer to live at home and to work at Fort Polk. Along with my work there, I preached almost every Sunday in some church in the area. One of those churches where I preached, Middle Creek Baptist Church, asked me to preach a revival for them that summer. Each night of the revival, before the service began, we participated in an old custom that a lot of churches in the area practiced. We had what they called "grove prayer meetings." Each of the age groups would meet separately for a time of prayer, and I met with the men to pray.

One night as we prayed, I squatted down on the ball of my right foot for an extended period of prayer. The next day, the calf on my right leg was sore. I didn't think much about it, but it kept getting sorer for the next several days. What I didn't know at the time was that I was having my first attack of an ancient disease that runs in my mother's family, I had developed phlebitis. What caused this in my family? I don't know. It could be that our blood has super-clotting tendencies, or that the valves in our veins don't work well, allowing the blood to pool, clot and become infected. Whatever the reason, the disease stretches back through every generation of my family on my mom's side as far back as I can find out.

I was dating Danielle at the time, and the next Saturday she and I, along with her cousin Rosa Herrington and her boyfriend (and soon-to-be husband) John Skinner, decided to go to Kisatchie Falls. Kisatchie Falls wasn't much as far as waterfalls are concerned, but they were about the best we could find around where we lived in West Central Louisiana.

We carried a picnic, walked in the shallow water, and then went swimming in a deeper hole in the creek. I was still limping a little on my leg but tried to hide it from them. I walked out into the water until it almost reached my chin, and then I felt a heaviness on my chest and began to have difficulty breathing. I didn't say anything to them about it, but I immediately got out of the water, sat down beside the creek, and tried to put my head down between my legs to overcome the dizziness I was experiencing.

That's the last thing that I remember before I passed out. When I finally came to, everyone was gathered over me and trying to talk to me. I was able to tell them about my difficulty breathing, so they put me into the car and carried me to the nearest hospital in Many, Louisiana. The folks at the hospital x-rayed my chest and found that a blood clot had moved from my leg to my lungs (a pulmonary embolism). They immediately started me on blood thinners, and I developed pneumonia.

As soon as I was able, my doctor, Dr. N. U. Booker, sent me to Methodist Hospital in Houston to see a doctor who was making waves with his treatment of the heart and circulatory system, Dr. Michael DeBakey. Dr. De-Bakey put me on bed rest and blood thinners and told me he didn't think surgery would be necessary. I stayed in the hospital for several days, and after Dr. DeBakey's last visit, accompanied by about 20 young doctors who gathered around my bed, he patted me on the leg and sent me home. That pat on the leg by one of the world's greatest doctors brought me assurance. I have now been on blood thinners and support stockings for over 50 years, have had a few minor rounds with the legs, but have never thrown another clot and have been blessed to do pretty much what I want to do most of my life.

Pulmonary embolisms can cause death. They are especially dangerous if they hit you while you are in the water like I was. I could have easily passed out while I was in the water and drowned that day if I hadn't been able to make it to the bank. So, I consider myself very blessed that none of those things happened.

It is of some value having an incident like that when you are a young man. It shows you that you are not invincible. I have lived more than 50 years since that day, and I see every one of those years as a gift of God. I am very grateful to God who spared my life that day, let me share all of these years with my family, allowed me to pastor nine wonderful churches, and has enabled me to preach His Word for 50 more years! Every day of every year that we live is a sacred gift. May God help us be good stewards of these gifts.

The Bottom Is Sound

When I was growing up in Plainview, Louisiana, one of the significant dates on our yearly calendar was the Saturday before the third Sunday in August. That Saturday was Memorial Day at Prewitt's Chapel Cemetery. All of my folks who had died on Daddy's side of the family were buried in that cemetery. Each August we made our annual pilgrimage to the cemetery to pay our respects. We visited the graves, went inside the church for a memorial service, went to stand by the graves of family members for prayer, and then had a big dinner-on-the-grounds beneath the trees. The dinner was complemented by Ottis Brown's coffee made in an iron wash pot. I never did like coffee, but since it was a chance to act grownup, I sometimes would drink a little of that bitter brew.

On the way to the cemetery, my brothers and I always liked my dad to take the dirt road that ran from our house by Cleo Alford's. The reason we wanted this route was that it had two fords on the road. At the bottom of the hill by Cleo Alford's, there was no culvert or bridge over the branch that crossed the road. You forded the shallow stream. The bottom was firm with a layer of sand on top. It was a lot of fun and a real attraction if we had any of our city cousins visiting us. The other ford on the road was right before you got to Leonard Slaughter's house. It too was a shallow stream with a good bottom, and wagons and cars had been fording the stream there for years.

Eventually, some energetic politician insisted that the streams ought to have culverts instead of fords, although the bottoms were still sound. So in the name of progress, they did away with one of our sources of entertainment and one of our links with the past. Today when we go that way, we no longer get to ford the streams.

And, my parents (K. C. and Reba Jones) no longer carry us to Prewitt's Chapel Cemetery. Both of them are now buried there. My dad made his final journey there in 1971, and my mom made her final journey there in 2007.

In John Bunyan's Pilgrim's Progress, two travelers, Christian and Hopeful, were on their journey to the City of God. As the City of God came into view, the two were separated from that shining city by a final dark river. Hopeful, as hope always does, led the way into that dark river. From the midst of the stream, he called back to

Christian on the bank of the river, "Be of good cheer, my brother, for I feel the bottom, and it is sound."

On the Saturday before the third Sunday in August, a lot of folks will go back to Prewitt's Chapel Cemetery for Memorial Day. My mom and dad forded those streams by Cleo Alford's and Leonard Slaughter's many times and always found the bottoms sound. And I believe that when they came at last to cross the final river, by the grace of God, they found the bottom sound. Those of us who loved them will remember and give thanks.

Learning from the Man in the Hat

Outside of AT&T Stadium in Arlington, Texas, there is a statue of a man dressed in a suit who is wearing a hat. It is a statue of Tom Landry. For 29 years, Tom Landry coached the Dallas Cowboys. He stood along the side-lines as players came and went. He was the constant that held the team together. In the early years, the challenges were enormous. He started with a squad of discards from other teams. Eddie LeBaron was his quarterback. Landry said that the snap from center was so bad that LeBaron would sometimes raise his hand before the snap to call for a fair catch.

In spite of poor records, the first Cowboys teams would always come sprinting onto the field for the start of the game. When someone asked Landry how he got the guys so fired up at the beginning of the game, he said that he gave them this speech in the locker room: "Men, the last 11 players out of the locker room are going to have to start the game."

Landry seldom displayed his emotions. He saw his lack of emotion as a matter of discipline and self-control. He said, "Leadership is a matter of having people look at you and gain confidence, seeing how you react. If you're in control, they're in control." The source of Landry's control was his faith and commitment to Jesus Christ. Blackie Sherrod wrote of Landry, "His unyielding faith and devout trust in God contributed to his strength. Not just contributed; it was his strength."

In the midst of his march to 13 division titles, five Super Bowls, and two Super Bowl trophies, Landry never lost his perspective on the most important things in life. He once said, "There is something more important than football—it is my relationship with Jesus Christ." That kind of balance and perspective made a significant impact upon countless people who observed Landry in action for many years.

Landry devoted a great deal of time to working with Bill Glass in prison ministries. He also supported the Fellowship of Christian Athletes. FCA Vice-President Kevin Harlan said, "I've heard it said, 'Preach Christ always, and, if necessary, use words.' I think Coach Landry lived that." I agree. I am grateful for the fun I had watching his teams and for the inspiration I received in watching his life.

Life's Last Slow Ride

When I was pastor of Highland Baptist Church in Shreveport, Louisiana, I preached the funeral of a friend and long-time member of the church. The next day I wrote the following:

When I drive around our town, I usually drive just as fast as the speed limit allows (give or take a few miles per hour). I have a lot of important things to do (or so it seems to me), and I am in a hurry to reach my next appointment.

Sometimes it is different, however. Sometimes I drive through town very, very slowly. These drives, which have occurred all too frequently this year, are when I am part of a procession of cars moving from the funeral home to the cemetery.

I am near the front of the procession. The body of our friend is in the hearse behind. Behind that is a family whose heart is breaking, for whom this whole day seems like a bad dream from which they are unable to awake.

Our slow, silent procession dramatizes the departure of our friend. The police stop all the traffic for us as we make our way, and they let us go through all the stop signs. They had never done that before as our friend made his way through town. It is a tribute paid to him for his final journey.

Along the way, we pass the businesses where he shopped and made his living. We pass the house where he lived and reared his family. It stands silent this day.

We drive slowly past our church building. That church was a place where he celebrated sacred events—his salvation, his wedding, the baptism of his children, his children's weddings, high moments with God, deep fellowship, and lasting relationships. We pass slowly.

On the hill beyond is the hospital. How many battles have been fought on that hill! He and his family won a lot of victories there—and suffered some painful losses. It was often the arena where he put into practice his faith.

And, finally, the cemetery. All of these slow journeys wind up here. "Each man starts with his very first breath. To devise shrewd means for outwitting death." None succeeds, of course. Eventually, we all make this trip.

Will these slow, sad journeys never end? Will they ever give way to triumphant alleluias?

The leaves of my Bible rustle in the wind as I stand beside the open grave and read a final word. Death seems so final, but the leaves of this Word are rustling with the rumor that it will not always be so. They rustle with the resurrection, victory, and life eternal.

A circle of friends, tearful embraces, lingering farewells. The journey back is made at regular speed.

Life is punctuated by these slow journeys. And the meaning of life is always made clearer when the punctuation has been added.

Making Judgments about Other People

Few days are more important in the National Football League than draft day. The decisions that are made will have a tremendous impact on the future of all the teams in the league for years to come. On draft day, teams make crucial decisions about which players to draft to play on their teams. In order to get ready for these days, the teams employ dozens of scouts.

Nowadays, it is a year-round job. They spread out over the United States watching football games and evaluating talent. Armed with stop-watches, speed guns, and video cameras, they assess foot speed, strength, quickness, and dozens of other traits. When all of this information has been compiled, they feed it into a computer, have dozens of experts check and recheck it, and then make their decisions.

With all of this expertise, you would think that it would be a foolproof method to get the best players for your team. However, that is not the case. Sometimes the number one draft choices don't pan out. They are dismal failures when they reach the NFL. When asked why that is the case, one executive said that injuries play a role in it, but more often it is a case of "wrong assessment." The experts just did not make the correct judgments. The next superstar didn't make it.

On the other hand, sometimes a player makes it that they did not expect to make it. The Most Valuable Player in the league in 1999 and 2001 was Kurt Warner, quarterback of the world champion St. Louis Rams. When he graduated from Northern Iowa in 1995, he was not drafted in the first round or the second round. In fact, he was not drafted at all. Instead of going to an NFL team, he went to the Iowa Barnstormers in the Arena Football League where he played for two years. From there he went to the European football league before coming to the NFL and stardom.

If the best judges in the world make such glaring mistakes, do you suppose that you and I are any better judges than they? The fact of the matter is that we are always making wrong assessments about people. We sometimes write people off as having little talent or ability. We later find out we were completely wrong. Why do we make such glaring errors? It's because we can see only on the outside of people. It's also because we are notoriously critical in our judgments.

Jesus made some outstanding draft picks for His team during His ministry. He saw great potential in unlikely people. May God help us be as sensitive and discerning as He.

Moving to a Higher Level in Your Life

The Ten-Tom Waterway connects the Tennessee River to the Tombigbee River in eastern Mississippi and makes shipping possible from the Gulf of Mexico all the way to the mouth of the Tennessee River and beyond. One of the things needed in order to make this shipping a reality is a series of locks and dams located on the waterway. When a boat arrives at a lock, it is faced with the formidable task of lifting itself ten to 20 feet straight up. Regardless of how powerful a boat may be, it does not have the power needed for such a task.

This is where the lock comes into play. The boat enters the lock, and the gate is closed behind the boat. The water begins flowing into the lock beneath the boat. As the water continues to flow, it gradually lifts the boat higher and higher until it has reached the new level. The gate is then opened, and the boat sails ahead on a higher level than before.

We often sail through life on one level, and there is a desperate need to move to a higher level. Life, with its weight of worry and care, presses down on us. We find ourselves moving on the same predictable level day after day. What can be done? We have no power to lift ourselves. We stand in need of some buoyant power beyond ourselves.

Sometimes the lift comes from times of private fellowship with God. In the midst of a busy day, we close out the routines of the world and shut ourselves up with God. The power of the Holy Spirit, like rivers of water, surrounds us. When we leave that time of fellowship with God, we embark on a higher level.

Or, sometimes the lift comes from times of public worship in fellowship with other Christians. We come to worship on one level. Often we are drawn by a grim sense of duty. Sometimes we come with no high expectations. Then, worship begins. We voice our songs of affirmation and assurance. We stand alongside persons who struggle with the same problems we do. We are stirred by prayers. We express our allegiance through giving. Our hearts are opened to the quickening power of the Word of God. We deepen our commitments. Gradually, imperceptibly, the waters of life surround us and lift us. We are drawn upward. The time comes when the final benediction is spoken, and we move on. But we do not move on at the same level. We have been lifted. We move on at a higher level.

Experience the power of God in your life. Let Him lift you to a new level!

My Honeymoon Sunburn

In 1968, Danielle and I got married in Pine Grove Baptist Church in Peason, Louisiana. I was the pastor at Pine Grove, and she was the pianist. It marked the first and last time that I ever ran off with the pianist of a church of which I was pastor. We went on our honeymoon to New Orleans. Then, we decided that we wanted to go to the beach. At this time, America had been discovered, but Gulf Shores and Destin had not. Around home, when most people wanted to go to the beach, they went to Galveston, Texas. So, that is where we headed.

As we prepared to go to the beach, I told Danielle that I had a tendency to sunburn. She said, "I will put suntan oil on you, and you won't have a thing to worry about" (Sunscreen had not yet been invented). So, I put suntan oil on me, and, on a warm, hazy day, I carried my lily-white body out to the beach where I lay on a towel from ten to two, with nothing but suntan oil between the sun and me. I occasionally heard a sizzling sound, sort of like bacon frying, but did not realize until I got inside and looked at myself in the mirror that I had been the one sizzling.

We went to a movie that night, and as I sat in the theater, I would occasionally feel a chill. By the time we got back to the room, I was running a pretty high fever from my sunburn. The next morning when I put my feet on the floor, I felt excruciating pain. When I stood up, the pressure stretched the skin around my ankles, and it nearly killed me. My ankles and most of the skin that had been exposed to the sun were covered with clear blisters. The only way that I could stand to get around the room was to get down on my hands and knees and crawl around the room.

As Danielle observed me crawling around the room, the one who only a few days before had solemnly promised to love me in sickness as in health, couldn't help but laugh a little. I must confess that I failed to see the humor in the situation, and this led to the exchange of a few cross words.

Because of my condition, we soon packed our bags, cut our honeymoon short, and headed home. When I told my story at home, my own brothers thought it was a little funny. At least my mother was sympathetic (Thank the Lord for mothers). I am now a lot older, and a good bit wiser than I was then, and Danielle and I have done in our marriage what all couples do in good marriages. We have come to understand each other better and have reached many understandings and compromises. I care absolutely nothing about a bronze tan, and she loves the sun and a tan. She is free to go to the beach as long as she likes. If I go down to the beach at all these days, I wear jeans, shirts, caps, stand under an umbrella, and, as soon as it is socially acceptable, I head to the refuge of a motel room, bookstore, or restaurant! I no longer crawl around on the floor of our motel room, and we exchange very few cross words these days.

People of Our Word

A few years ago Jim Greenlee took office as U. S. Attorney for the northern district of Mississippi. At the ceremony in which Greenlee was installed in this office, Greenlee's brother-in-law Robert Whitwell spoke. Whitwell described Greenlee as "a man of his word." He added that Greenlee tries to be like their father-in-law, the late Fletcher Veazey. Whitwell added, "When Fletcher Veazey said Santa Claus was coming on the Fourth of July, you'd better hang up a sock."

I'd say that it is great for a person to have that kind of credibility. Many do not have that kind of devotion to honesty and telling the truth. I heard of a man of questionable reputation who was placed on the witness stand at a trial. He was asked, "Do you promise to tell the truth, the whole truth, and nothing but the truth?" He responded, "Sure, I'll be glad to try anything once."

Jesus spoke to the people of His day who were often shading and distorting the truth. According to the predominant religious tradition of the time, if an oath was taken on some things it was considered "binding." If it was taken on other things it was considered "non-binding." Experts on the religious law used their knowledge of "binding" and "non-binding" oaths to take advantage of people who were not experts. Jesus suggested another way. He said, "Why don't you let your 'yes' be 'yes,' and your 'no' be 'no?'" Or, simply tell the truth. Don't try to obscure the truth behind a maze of legal jargon.

The ultimate model for this kind of dependability and credibility is God Himself. God has given us His Word. Within that Word, He has made many promises. Every promise of God is absolutely dependable.

When we come to follow Christ, the pledge to tell the truth is at the heart of that commitment. We sometimes say, "He is a man of his word." I heard an interesting version of that saying which was used of a man. It said, "He is a man of his word because he is a man of His Word." A commitment to His Word should automatically result in our being people of our word.

Receiving an LUI

One of the most serious driving offenses is a DUI—Driving Under the Influence. When a person is driving while under the influence of drugs or alcohol, he is a menace on the highway. His vision is impaired, his judgment is clouded, and his reaction time is slowed. Persons who "Drive Under the Influence" wreak havoc on the roadways of our nation and leave in their wake a tangled trail of broken lives.

While a DUI is a serious offense, I would like to offer a word of commendation for an LUI—Living Under the Influence. When a person is living under the influence of the Spirit of God, he is a blessing to everyone he meets on the road of life.

Paul once drew a sharp distinction between these two types of influences. He wrote to the Ephesians, "Do not get drunk on wine, which leads to debauchery. Instead, be filled with the Spirit" (Eph. 5:18). Instead of being filled with "spirits," we should be filled with the Spirit. Whereas the first leads to "debauchery," the latter leads to a life of blessing.

Often, we have not been clear on the role of the Holy Spirit. Dorothy Sayers told the story of a Japanese gentleman who was discussing the mysterious concept of the Trinity in Christianity. A friend tried to explain the doctrine to him by reading the account of Jesus' baptism in which you have the Son being baptized, the voice of the Father speaking, and the presence of the Spirit descending as a dove. The Japanese man responded, "I understand the Honorable Father and the Honorable Son, but I do not at all understand the Honorable Bird."

According to Scripture, at the time we accept Christ as Savior, our bodies become the temple of the Holy Spirit. He comes to dwell within us.

As a result of His presence, then we are to Live Under the Influence. The Spirit should influence our decisions and our values. He should influence our attitudes and our pursuits. The Spirit comes to empower us in our weaknesses and to control our temperaments. As we allow Him to influence our lives, He begins to produce the fruits of the Spirit—things like love, joy, peace, longsuffering, gentleness, goodness, faith, meekness, and temperance.

One of our problems is that we often live life without allowing Him to influence us much. For His influence to be what it ought to be, our daily prayer should be that He would fill us and control us.

An old black preacher was challenging some young preacher friends. He said, "I want to remind you that God not only appoints; He also anoints." As He anoints us with His Spirit, He empowers us to live the Christian life.

A DUI is a serious offense. An LUI is a wonderful blessing. I encourage you today to Live Under the Influence of the Spirit of God.

One of God's Favorites

In an elementary school where my wife Danielle once served as librarian, she hosted all of the elementary classes sometime during the week. In one of those classes, there was a very rambunctious little boy named Jared. He was so hyper that he was forever getting into trouble. Most of the teachers dreaded to see him coming.

Danielle has always liked high-energy boys and usually was pretty successful in controlling them. One of her methods was to take a boy like that and involve him in some way—let him hand out the papers or stack the books, or something. It was a way of channeling all of that energy. Using that method, for most of the year she was quite successful in keeping Jared's conduct within acceptable limits. He relished his role as a leader and looked forward to coming to the library every week.

But one week, Jared came into the library exceeding even Danielle's limits of acceptable behavior. As a corrective, she gave him no special privileges that day and had him sit in a chair by himself, somewhat removed from the rest of the class. Thrust into this new situation, he sat there pouting, not looking at any of the books she had placed before him. After a while, she went over to him and asked, "Jared, what's wrong?" He looked at her and said with a quiver in his voice, "And I thought I was one of your favorites."

I suppose that is always a difficult experience—to think that you are someone's favorite only to discover that it's not quite what you thought. Why, it's enough to make you question whether the person likes you at all.

In some ways, it works like that with God and us. The Bible declares that we are God's favorites. We are created in His image. He has declared His special interest in us. But sometimes there are events that occur that make us question our status with God. In fact, when difficult experiences come, we may wonder whether He loves us at all.

I read about a woman who was involved in a fender-bender at a busy street intersection. The accident left the front right fender of her new automobile badly crumpled. She was especially upset because she knew how much this car meant to her husband. Already, she was beginning to dread telling him what had happened.

When she was able to collect her thoughts, she began going through the glove compartment looking for the insurance papers, car title, etc. As she was looking through these papers, she saw a note card in her husband's handwriting. She took the card out and read the words he had written there: "In case you have an accident, remember, it's you I love and not the car."

And that is the way God feels toward us. When we really mess up in our lives, God still loves us. That doesn't change. I like the way one old Christian summed up the blessings of his life. He said, "I'll tell you something, The Lord has been partial to me all my life." So, He has to all of us!

Practicing Our Faith

A group of folks was talking about a mutual friend who lived in a distant city. One of them remembered that it was the friend's birthday, so they decided to call him and sing "Happy Birthday" over the telephone. They dialed the number, and as soon as there was an answer at the other end, they launched into a spirited rendition of "Happy Birthday." When they had finished singing, there was a period of silence, and then the man on the other end of the line gave his name. It was then that they discovered that they had called the wrong number. They apologized profusely for singing to him. The man who had been serenaded said, "Don't worry about it. You folks need the practice.

A lot of us need the practice. Not just with our singing but with our faith. The fact of the matter is that many of us talk a better game than we play. Our practice often does not match up to our profession. Someone has said that one of life's biggest disappointments is discovering that the guy who writes the advertisements for the bank is not the guy who writes the loans. Often there is some distance between what the ad says and what a business will actually do. The same is true of our Christian lives.

One man said, "On a good day, I can make five or six good resolutions before breakfast. If I had realized only 2% of these in the past year, people would be blinded by my halo."

We recognize our need to grow and mature. We know that we need to make progress and often resolve to do so. But translating the resolutions into action is the point at which we stumble.

That indeed was not the case with Jesus. John Killinger said that it is impossible to drive the thinnest blade between what He taught and how He acted. What He said was what He did. He challenges us with inspiring words and with a consistent life. That gives His witness a profound impact on our lives.

How often we weaken our witness by the lack of consistency in our lives. We profess kindness and love but act out of insensitivity and selfishness. We talk of holiness and commitment but reflect worldliness and superficiality.

Identical twins pursued different careers. One of them became a medical doctor. The other surrendered to preach and earned his doctorate in theology. After completing their separate degrees, both brothers moved to the same town—one to practice medicine and the other to pastor a local church. Because the two men looked exactly alike, people were constantly confused about which one was which. One day a woman met one of the men on a city sidewalk and was unsure about which one he was. She asked, "Are you the brother who preaches?" "No," he responded, "I am the brother who practices."

I am grateful for those who preach. I am even more grateful for those who practice.

Preaching With Peanuts

Several years after I moved from the pastorate of Highland Baptist Church in Shreveport to the pastorate of First Baptist Church in Booneville, Mississippi, I received a very nice sympathy card from my friends Bill and Alene Duncan in Shreveport. The front of the card said, "With thoughts of deepest sympathy." I was very touched but also puzzled. Why the sympathy card? I opened the card and the message inside, which had been slightly altered, said, "Thinking of you and hoping you find comfort in the lifetime of special memories of Peanuts cartoons!"

Some former church members recognized a loss when they see one. Having heard me preach for several years, they knew how often I had summoned Charlie Brown, Lucy, Linus, Snoopy, and company to make a point. Now that Charles Schultz was retiring and drawing no more strips, they were concerned about exactly what I would find to illustrate my sermons and articles in the days ahead.

Well, I must admit that I had come to lean pretty heavily on these small characters. They always had a way of illustrating a truth with a touch of humor—one of my favorite approaches.

They illustrated the need for a more profound knowledge of the Bible. Take the time Linus let out a big sigh, and Lucy said, "Stop that stupid sighing."

Then, the following exchange: Linus: "There's nothing wrong with sighing." Lucy: "There is if it bugs someone." Linus: It's scriptural." Lucy: "It's what?" Linus: "Likewise the Spirit helps us in our weakness, for we do not know how to pray as we ought, but the Spirit himself intercedes for us with sighs too deep for words. Romans, eighth chapter."

The final frame shows Lucy saying to herself, "I don't know. . . I'm either going to have to slug him or start going back to Sunday School."

Or, take the time Charlie Brown talked about his feeling of emptiness and lack of purpose. Linus said, "It's just the way it is, Charlie Brown. We inherit it from our families." Charlie responded, "That's always been the trouble with our family. We have too much heredity."

Or, they sometimes put the finger squarely upon our vanity and blindness to our faults—especially in the person of Lucy. In one strip, Lucy was looking at herself in the mirror. As she did so, Charlie Brown was lecturing her: "And besides, never forget that beauty is only skin deep." Lucy responded, "I deny that! My beauty is not only on the surface, it goes down deep. . . layer after layer after layer. Yes, sir," she said as she looked at herself again in the mirror, "I have very thick beauty."

When I was growing up, my brother Wayne and I had a particular ritual. Each afternoon when we would get in from school, we would take the paper, kneel in front of the sofa, spread the paper on the sofa, open it to the comics, and read them. One of those comics was "Peanuts." I have read it every day since then. After Schultz's retirement and death, I missed new adventures, but the good news is that I have many files of old ones that I will continue to mine. Thank you, Charles Schultz, for your help and partnership in seeing the truth and in communicating the truth.

Raggedy Anns in a Barbie Doll World

While we were on vacation one summer, I saw a sign in a gift shop that said, "I'm just a Raggedy Ann in a Barbie Doll world." In many ways, it is a Barbie Doll world. The media constantly push the rich and beautiful people of the world. Like it or not, for many folks, their models for life are the beautiful people that dominate television and magazines. The only problem with that is that most of us do not look like these people. We do not have their money nor their opportunities. Why, it's enough to make you feel like a Raggedy Ann in a Barbie Doll world! It can make you feel of little value.

An old story tells of a confirmed bachelor who became good friends with an old maid. Gradually, he began to think about the possibility of their getting married. He finally got up the courage to mention the subject to her. He said, "Why don't we get married?" She responded, "Huh, who'd have you and me?"

The fact of the matter is that God has made you exactly the way you are and has invested you with significant gifts. The gifts may be fewer, and they may be different from those possessed by others, but never underestimate their importance. Observation shows that the materials used are not the determining factor in great art. Some produce great art with simple materials. And God can bring forth masterpieces from simple gifts that are yielded to His hand.

The gifts that you have may be of critical importance in the accomplishment of God's purpose and plan in the world, even if those gifts may seem small and insignificant. I read of a man who was involved in many great musical productions. His responsibility? He was a professional page-turner for pianists. And there may be some people around who need some help when they have reached their last note. The faithful use of your gift may be critical in the life of someone around you.

When our lives and gifts are yielded to God, then it is always amazing what God can do with them. I like the prayer that one woman prayed over her life. She prayed, "Lord, treat me like a checker. Move me wherever you want me to go." When we yield ourselves to God, He can use Raggedy Anns to make an enormous impact on a Barbie Doll world.

Relating to Our Past

Finding the right relationship to our history is always a challenge. One of our dangers is becoming so enamored with our memories that we spend all of our time yearning for a bygone era and not being good stewards of the opportunities here and now.

Nostalgia has been defined as remembering the campfires but forgetting the smoke in your eyes. We sometimes do that with the past. A classic example of that is the Israelites who were on their way from Egypt to the Promised Land. As they made their way across the wilderness, they began idealizing life in distant Egypt. They burned out on manna and began remembering the meat, cucumbers, leeks, onions and garlic in Egypt.

They longed for those wonderful meals and began talking about returning to Egypt.

The "Back to Egypt Committee" is often one of the most active committees in the church. It longs for the good old days when everyone loved the Lord, attended church, and did what was right.

The problem with the Israelites is that they forgot about the slavery and terrible persecution in Egypt. Their memory was very selective. The idealized past became an impossible competitor with the reality of the present.

In the same way, there has never been a golden era in the life of the church when everybody loved the Lord, attended church, and did what was right. Our sins and shortcomings have been present in every age.

The other extreme against which we have to guard in relating to the past is ignoring it completely. One man gave this bit of advice about lending money to other people. He said, "Never lend money. It is dangerous because it causes amnesia in those who receive it." We also suffer from historical amnesia. We tend to forget everything that has been given to us. Amnesia of any sort is always tragic.

If there is no memory of the past, there is no gratitude for all that we owe to those who have gone before us. We are tremendously blessed by the sacrifices of persons who have preceded us in the church.

When we remember the past, we learn from the past. Mark Twain said that history does not repeat itself, but it does rhyme. The events are not the same but often there are similarities from which we can learn.

Remembering also fosters unity. Memories have been called the "epoxy of humanity." As we recall shared memories, there is a mystical bonding of those who remember.

John Graves said that a person who cultivates his roots too much is like a potato—more root than plant. But the one who cultivates his roots too little soon withers and dies because a healthy root system is vital to plants and people. We have to find the right balance between roots and shoots.

Residents of the Neutral Strip

I am a native of the Neutral Strip. Let me explain.

In 1803, the Unites States bought Louisiana from France. This territory, known as the Louisiana Purchase, included "all the land drained by the Mississippi River." When the Americans asked the French about the exact western boundary of this land, the French were very vague. A definite boundary of Louisiana had not been determined. The Spaniards, who controlled Texas at the time, considered the western boundary of Louisiana to be the Red River. The Americans claimed it to be the Sabine River. Finally, in 1806, the American general James Wilkinson met with the Spanish commander to work out an agreement. Since the two could not decide whether the western boundary of Louisiana was the Red River or the Sabine River, the area between these two rivers was declared to be a neutral strip.

From 1806 to 1820, this area was referred to as "The Neutral Strip." It soon attracted all kinds of people who were eager to take advantage of a land without law enforcement. It was not until 1820 that the western boundary of Louisiana was set at the Sabine River and the Neutral Strip faded into history.

My ancestors lived in this neutral strip of land, and I was born and reared there myself. Although I was born a long time after "The Neutral Strip" was gone, it has had its effect on me. I keep detecting this strong streak in me that wants to remain neutral. I often find it easier to duck decisions than make them.

I am in sympathy with the young baseball umpire who was calling his first game. Unfortunately, the game was close, the fans vocal, and the managers menacing. It was the bottom of the ninth, the score was tied, there were two outs, and the bases were loaded. The count on the batter was 1-1. The pitcher reared back and hummed a fast ball toward the plate. The batter did not swing, and the young umpire roared, "TWO!" With that, both managers came running toward the plate, stood on either side of the rookie umpire and demanded in unison, "Two what?" The young umpire took a deep breath and said, "Too close to call."

It is tempting in life for us to refuse to make a decision--remain neutral. The problem is that life keeps demanding a decision, especially about our allegiance to Christ and our obedience to His Lordship.

Those who have made the most impact for Christ have been those who have been willing to abandon the "Neutral Strip" and take a definite stand. Moses was such a man. Dwight L. Moody said that when Moses first undertook the task of delivering Israel from slavery (by killing the Egyptian who was mistreating the Israelite) he "looked this way and that" (Ex. 2:12). But after his encounter with God at the burning bush, he looked only one way, God's way. That's the way we ought to look. If you are currently living in the "Neutral Strip," I encourage you to make a move to the land of His Lordship!

Saying Goodbye

One of the first words that children learn is the word "bye." The word is simple because it has one syllable and begins with a good, hard vowel. "Bye" is an easy word to say. But I have also discovered across the years that "bye" is one of the most difficult words to say. It is not difficult because it is hard to pronounce but because of the emotions that it stirs.

Funerals are often marked by the most wrenching "goodbyes." This is a goodbye that is being said for the final time (at least in this life). This goodbye is very difficult and is often marked by great emotion.

When I first began preaching, I used to have a great fear of funerals. The thing that I feared was that I would cry when I stood by the casket to hear a family say its goodbyes. I was fearful that my tears would be a sign of weakness and frail faith.

I have since changed my mind about that. If someone could stand by and hear a family say goodbye to a loved one without being moved by it, then that would be something to be concerned about.

I have heard all kinds of goodbyes across the years. Some are charged with emotion. Others are restrained. Sometimes there are many words. Sometimes there are none.

When I served as pastor of Highland Baptist Church in Shreveport, I was strangely moved by a goodbye that I heard at a funeral. Doris Burrows, a long-time member of the church, died. Doris suffered from congestive heart failure. When the end drew near, she decided that she would rather go to the Father's house from her home than from the hospital. So, in what is a rather rare occurrence these days, she lived out the final days of her life at home.

Sitters and her family ministered to her. One of those members of her family was not a relative. She was a wonderful black woman named Charlie Mae. For 35 years, Charlie Mae had worked for the family. She had been more than a family maid; she had been a family member. It was altogether fitting that when I looked to where the family was seated that day for the funeral I saw Charlie Mae seated with them.

At the conclusion of the service, the friends filed by the open casket. Then the family. After most had said their goodbyes, Charlie Mae said her goodbye. She must have been thinking about exactly what she would say.

She said it briefly and in a low voice that probably only I heard. She said, "Sleep on Mrs. Doris, and take your rest. We all loved you, but Jesus loves you best."

And I shed more than one tear and was unashamed.

Sharing the Word with Everyone

A missionary once told about an African man to whom he had given a copy of the Bible. The African was deeply grateful for the Bible and thanked the missionary again and again for the gift. Several months later the missionary saw the man again. The missionary was puzzled because the Bible that he had given the man was battered and torn. It looked as though many of the pages were missing.

The missionary said, "I am disappointed by your treatment of the Bible I gave you. I assumed you wanted it and would take care of it."

The man responded, "It is the finest gift I have ever received. It is such a wonderful book that I gave a page from the book to my father and a page to my mother. Then I gave a page to everyone in my village."

What a testimony to the power of the Word of God! There is something so compelling about this Word that it causes you to want to give it away, to share it with everyone around you.

That missionary impulse has been part of the church since the beginning. The church at Antioch caught a vision for sharing the gospel with the entire world and dispatched Paul and Barnabas to Asia Minor. They believed that Jesus Christ cared for those people and that they needed to hear the gospel.

We sometimes lose our vision for sharing the gospel with the whole world. We have this way of categorizing everything. We are "over here" with God, and they are "over there." We see ourselves as the good guys, and they are the bad guys. We have on the white hats and they have on the black hats. Jesus undoubtedly would want to spend His time with us because we are the good guys with the white hats.

But when Jesus Christ was on earth, do you know what the big problem was? They couldn't keep Him away from the guys with the black hats. He just wouldn't put on the white hat and stay where He belonged. He was always out there with the bad guys, just like he loved them and cared for them and wanted to eat supper with them.

We need to look again at the life of Jesus and look at people the way He looked at them. Then we need to look again at our world. We need to catch an enlarged vision of all those in our world who need to know Christ as Savior.

Stand Up for Jesus

When I was pastor of Pine Grove Baptist Church in Peason, Louisiana, one of our former music directors would occasionally come back to visit us for one of our worship services. His name was Carah Coburn. The "ah" ending to his name was, in typical North Louisiana fashion, transformed into a hard "ee" sound, and he was called "Carree Coburn." Carah loved to sing, and he especially loved to lead singing. When Carah came to visit with us, everyone at the worship service, including Carah, expected us to invite him to lead singing. So one evening when he showed up for the evening worship service, I asked him to direct the music. He told me that he felt unqualified to do so, but when I insisted, he pulled out of his pocket a list of hymn numbers and gave them to Danielle who was playing the piano that night.

In the Baptist Hymnal of those days, there were two versions of the hymn, "Stand Up for Jesus." One was the traditional version, and the other version had the same lyrics, but the words were set to a more militant tune. Carah did not know that there were two versions of the hymn in the hymnal. So, that evening he selected the number for the more militant version but had in mind our singing the traditional version. When Danielle played the introduction to the militant version, he shot a startled glance in her direction but figured that she would get straightened out once he began singing.

After the introduction, he began singing the traditional version of the hymn, and Danielle began playing the militant version. I have seen this happen sometimes in other hymn selections, and generally, after the first few words, everyone would stop, and we would all get on the same page. Not this night. Carah would not stop, and Danielle would not stop. It resulted in an unforgettable musical experience. Danielle thought it was Carah's responsibility to stop, and she did not want to embarrass him by stopping herself. Carah evidently thought that Danielle didn't know how to play the piano, and he didn't want to stop and embarrass her by pointing it out. So, we plowed on.

If you focused on what Danielle was playing, it sounded like Carah couldn't carry a tune, and if you focused on what Carah was singing, it sounded like Danielle was just banging on the piano. The people didn't know what to do. Some of them tried halfheartedly to sing but found it difficult to know what tune to use. It really put me on the spot because Danielle was my wife, and I wanted to support her. Carah was a guest, and I wanted to support him. I wound up splitting my time. I would try to sing with her a little while, and then I would try to sing with him a little while.

As we came to the end of the first verse, I had some hopes that this would mark the end of the song, but no such luck. As we came down the homestretch of the first verse, Carah took a deep breath and headed into the second lap. The farther we went, the more forceful Carah was in singing, and the more militant Danielle was in playing. The same thing happened at the end of the second verse. We headed into the third and, mercifully, final verse of the hymn. I have sung many hymns in church services, but of all the hymns that I have ever sung that was the longest one by far.

By the time we had reached the end of the hymn, we were all so demoralized that everyone had quit trying to sing, and the only two things that you could hear were Carah's singing and Danielle's playing. When it was finally over, Carah was drenched in perspiration. He just shook his head and collapsed onto the front pew exhausted. That's the way I felt, but it was time for me to preach, so I summoned all of my strength to "stand up for Jesus," and make my way to the pulpit. I never mentioned the song but went straight to my sermon.

This marked the last time that Carah ever came to visit with us at the church while I was there and the last time that he ever led music for us. I guess he was waiting for us to get a new pianist before he came back.

You will hear a lot of tunes in the days ahead. Choose the one that you use carefully, but the most important thing is not the tune you use but the stand you take. I encourage you, regardless of the pressures or distractions, to "Stand Up for Jesus!"

The Challenge of Flexibility

One of the most significant challenges that a pastor faces is the challenge of flexibility. Ministry has an incredible variety of demands that it makes. One minute you can be visiting some folks in the hospital who are welcoming into their family a new baby. The next minute you might walk into a room where a family is preparing to say goodbye to a long-loved member of that family. You move from celebration to mourning in the space of a few minutes. Or, you might finish a wedding where a young couple is pledging their lifelong love to each other and then go to meet with a couple that is considering severing the final fragile bonds that unite them.

I'll tell you one of the most abrupt challenges to my flexibility that I ever faced. I had just finished studying my sermon for that Sunday morning and was walking into the church building for Sunday School. As I rounded the corner, I met a woman and her daughter who were both looking frightened and desperate. The mother blurted out to me that she and her husband Frank (not his real name) had been having trouble. They had been separated for several days and that Frank was at the front of the church with a gun.

I told them to go to my office, and I went walking out to the front of the church where Frank was standing beside his pickup truck. When I approached him, he began telling me how badly his wife had been treating him. He said that he had had all that he was going to take and that he had decided to kill himself. He took a step toward his truck where his pistol was lying on the front seat. I put my hands on his shoulder and said, "No, Frank, you don't want to do that." He said, "Preacher, don't you lay a hand on me."

With that, I started backing slowly away from him toward the back of the truck. I thought that if he grabbed the gun and started shooting, I could duck behind the truck. As I back-pedaled, I kept talking to him. As I spoke, he quit reaching toward the gun and began talking some more about his problems. I told him everything I knew and a couple of things I wasn't sure of, and gradually his demeanor softened. He began walking toward me and said, "Look, preacher, I don't have a gun. Let's talk."

And so we stood in the parking lot talking until it was almost time for worship. He finally said, "You don't have to worry, preacher, I'm not going to cause any problem here at church." And then he got into his truck and drove away.

I went running toward my office, grabbed my Bible, and made it to the sanctuary just as the choir was entering. Getting into a frame of mind for worship was a struggle that Sunday morning. I sat in my pulpit chair emotionally drained and distracted. I don't remember what I preached, but God made good on His promise that when we are caught in a crisis "it shall be given you in that same hour what you shall speak" (Matt. 10:19).

And God will give you the strength that you need for the challenges that you face. The challenges often come fast and furiously, but God is the same yesterday, today, and forever. You can trust Him. May God grant you the grace and flexibility that you need for life's incredible variety of demands!

Stormy Weather

For many years, every morning as I got ready to go to work I would listen to the stock market report on National Public Radio. Before they would give the figures for the previous day, they would give you a hint about what to expect. They introduced the segment by playing one of two tunes--"We're in the Money," or "Stormy Weather."

Stormy weather is a part of the pattern of stock markets and climate. According to the National Weather Service, at any given moment 2,000 thunderstorms are in progress in the world. Now that is a lot of stormy weather!

When those storms come where we live, they have a way of stirring up our fears. I heard of a woman who was very much afraid of such storms. As a thunderstorm was sweeping over her house with rain, wind, and lightning, she said to her husband, "The house is going to blow away." He said, "Don't worry; we're only renting." It is doubtful that such an observation was very reassuring.

Stormy weather is not only a part of our weather patterns, but it is also a part of the pattern of life. Life may sail along on calm seas and under sunny skies for a long time, but sooner or later storms will come. They come in all shapes and varieties. They come in our family life. They come on our jobs. They come with our health. One old preacher advised some young colleagues, "Whenever you are preaching, remember that everyone out there is either in a storm, has just come out of a storm, or is heading for a storm."

We respond to storms in all kinds of ways. That response reveals who we are. In the Bible, there are the accounts of three men who were caught in storms at sea. One of the men was Jonah. Jonah was running from God when God overtook him with a storm on the Mediterranean Sea. Jonah was sleeping the sleep of denial, but God confronted him with his sin in the storm that tossed his boat. As a result of that, Jonah was tossed overboard where he was forced to encounter God.

Paul was also caught in a storm on the Mediterranean Sea. He was not running from God; he was a prisoner because of his allegiance to God. He was being sent to Rome to stand trial before the Caesar. When the ship on which he was sailing was caught in a prolonged storm, Paul responded with faith. He was a dynamic witness to his fellow passengers about the presence and power of God.

Jesus was also caught in a storm. As He crossed the Sea of Galilee, He was asleep in the boat. His was not the sleep of denial; it was the sleep of peace. Jesus awoke, stretched forth His hands, and brought peace to the sea and to the hearts of His disciples.

He continues to do that. Sooner or later you will encounter "stormy weather," When you do, I encourage you to trust the One who left us the legacy of His peace!

The Alteration Shop

There's an old story about some mischievous boys who decided to have some fun at their pastor's expense. They got together and did what boys should never do. They took their pastor's Bible and glued some of the pages together. The results were dramatic. The next Sunday their pastor got up to preach on the creation of man and woman in Genesis 2. He was reading the text about the creation, and when he flipped the page, he turned all the way to the account of Noah's building the ark in Genesis 6.

This is what he read, "And with the rib, which the Lord God had taken from man, made he a woman and she [turn page] was three hundred cubits long, fifty cubits wide, and thirty cubits high." With that, the old preacher paused and said, "Well, I don't rightly remember reading that before, but it just goes to prove that other verse of

Scripture by the psalmist who said, "I am fearfully and wonderfully made."

Well, sometimes I feel that I am fearfully and wonderfully made. I hate to cast any aspersions on the Lord's handiwork, but I am afraid that He may have been distracted as He was creating me and placed on me some arms and legs that are entirely too short. I have come to terms with their length, but the clothing makers of this world have not. The end result is that I can seldom buy anything off the rack that fits. The sleeves and legs invariably are too long. When faced with this recurring dilemma, I am forced to carry the clothes to someone to make some changes. The changes made to clothes are called "alterations." For a price, you can get legs of pants and sleeves of coats altered to fit.

I wish it were easier to make some alterations to myself. I tried hanging from a tree limb one time to make my arms longer, but the results were disappointing. I never could figure out anything to try on the legs. Making significant changes inside of us is also difficult. In fact, change is always hard for us, but change is inescapably tied to growth. Growing things change. Someone has said that the conversion of a soul is the miracle of a moment; the building of a saint is the task of a lifetime. There is no end to that process. Every year should bring growth and change.

Morton Kelsey once stood before a giant redwood tree that had celebrated 3,500 birthdays. He noted that the tree stands nearly 300 feet high and is 100 feet around. It is 30 feet in diameter. But he noted, "Here is the most amazing fact: it is still growing! Each year it adds 500 more board feet to its trunk."

The size and shape of the tree are experiencing ongoing alterations. In the same way, we need to experience continuing alterations. Christ is at work through His church to bring about these kinds of changes in our lives. There are many metaphors for the church. Let me suggest another one. The church is "The Alteration Shop." God is at work in the big business of altering our lives.

The Big Impact of Small Things

Husbands and wives have many adjustments to make in their quest to live together in harmony. At no point is that ability to adjust put to the test more than when they sit down to watch television together. The great question is, "Which channel do we watch?" For some reason, wives prefer channels like the movie channel, the music channel, and (heaven forbid) even the shopping channel while avoiding perfectly good channels like the history channel, the sports channel, and the animal channel.

I suppose it's the last of those channels over which Danielle and I have the most sharply divided opinion. I enjoy a good animal feature, but she is a little too squeamish to enjoy some of the footage. I often resort to watching the channel while she is out of the room, but inevitably, just as she is walking through, there will be a close-up of a snake or an insect on the screen or some predator making a kill. Blake and I can always stir her up by saying, "Let's watch a few kills before bedtime."

In spite of her criticism of the channel, I can occasionally pick up some interesting information from the animal channel. Take this question for instance: "Which animal kills more people on the continent of Africa each year than any other animal?" I guessed the lion, but I was wrong. The animal that kills the second largest number of people is the hippopotamus. That is surprising, but when you think of the massive size of the hippo and how people are around them in bodies of water, I guess its understandable. But the animal that kills more people each year than any other was the most surprising of all because it is one of the smallest animals. It is the mosquito. More people are killed by diseases borne by the mosquito than are killed by attacks by larger animals.

We are impressed by the size and power of the larger things in life, but we often overlook the potential of the small and seemingly insignificant things. They have the potential for both good and bad.

Sometimes the small things have tremendously destructive potential. I had two beautiful pine trees that grew in my yard one time. Those trees endured powerful storms that swept through our town on many occasions. They survived stifling heat and bone-chilling cold. But eventually, both of those pine trees died. They died because a tiny pine beetle bored into the thin layer of wood that carries the life-giving moisture and nutrients to the rest of the tree. When this little pine beetle was joined by others of its kind, the needles of the pine trees soon turned brown, and both of them died.

Little sins have that power in our lives. Never underestimate their destructive potential.

On the other hand, small things have a great power for good in our lives. The small deed, the daily faithfulness, the kind word can all be used in powerful ways.

A kindergarten teacher has been defined as "a person who can make little things count." That is a valuable lesson that all of us could learn!

The Big Power of a Small Word

"If" is a word, but it has tremendous power and influence. Careful use of the word "if" can have an enormous impact on life. Sometimes we use the word as a club to hit ourselves over the head about previous mistakes. For example, "If only I had not made that bonehead decision." Or, "If only I had not said that." Of course, the fact of the matter is that we cannot change what has happened in the past. The poet wrote: "The moving finger writes, and having writ moves on. Nor all your tears, nor all your regrets can change a single line of it." To spend all of our time wishing that something had not happened only weakens us in our ability to cope with the consequences.

Sometimes we use the word "if" to excuse ourselves from some responsibility. For example, "If only I had the

training, I would be glad to teach a Sunday School class."
Or, "If only I had the talent, I would be glad to take that
position." We think of all the big things we could do if we
had specific abilities. The fact of the matter is that there
are a lot of smaller things that we could tackle that would
be well within the range of things that we could accomplish.

Sometimes we use the word "if" to try to make deals
with God. For example, we say, "Lord, if you will do this,
then I will do that." The result is that often we come across
as a salesman trying to make a good deal with God. In
the book of Daniel, there is the story of the three Hebrew
children who were threatened by the king with the fiery
furnace if they did not worship his golden image. They
responded, "If it be so, our God whom we serve is able to
deliver us. . . But if not, be it known unto thee, O king, that
we will not serve thy gods, nor worship the golden image
which thou hast set up."

In the Garden of Gethsemane, Jesus prayed, "O my
Father, if it be possible, let this cup pass from me: nevertheless not as I will, but as thou wilt." In a real sense, an
index of maturity in our lives is how far we have moved
from the "if" pole of life toward the "nevertheless" pole.
How about you? How far have you traveled?

The Chick Hearn Legacy

Chick Hearn died in 2002. Chick was the long-time broadcaster for the Los Angeles Lakers. He holds the record for broadcasting the most consecutive games. From Nov. 21, 1965, to Dec. 16, 2001, Chick broadcast 3,338 straight games. You have to admire a man who reports to work every day for 36 years.

While watching Lakers games broadcast on NBA television, I used to hear Chick's running commentary on the games. Since his analysis was intended for radio as well as for TV, he gave you a full account of what was going on.

Across his long career of broadcasting NBA games, Chick almost single-handedly supplied us with a whole new vocabulary to use in describing basketball. He was the first to use such expressions as slam dunk, finger roll, garbage time, and air ball.

He used some expressions that not only could be used to describe plays on the basketball court but could very well be used to describe the way we often live the Christian life. When a player was a tad slow, Chick would say, "He's so slow I saw him on an escalator yesterday, and a step passed him by." Sometimes we are that slow in the church to respond to the needs of a world that is changing around us. If we're not careful, it will pass us by, and our witness will be rendered ineffective.

It was Chick who described a shot that had no "touch" as being a "brick." If a player persisted in throwing up "bricks" throughout the game, Chick would say, "He's thrown up enough bricks to build a house." Our efforts to serve God are often like that. Our words are clumsy, and our actions may be insensitive. We throw up a lot of "bricks."

Or, take the way Chick described an attempt to make a fancy pass that failed to connect. He said, "He threw a hot dog pass, and the mustard came off and is all over the floor." Sometimes our attempts to do things that call attention to ourselves backfire on us. The results can be embarrassing.

Chick also had a way of affirming players. He liked an enthusiastic player. He sometimes said, "He's wound up like a toy on Christmas morning." Nothing like a little enthusiasm in the Christian life to help us do our best.

Or, Chick would speak admiringly of a good play made by a clutch player in a hot situation. He would say, "They go to their bread and butter man, who also delivers ice." You have to admire Christians who are like that. They are dependable and keep their cool even in very heated situations.

And then there was the way Chick would describe a game that had been put out of reach. He would say, "This game's in the refrigerator. The door's closed, the light's out, the eggs are cooling, the butter's getting hard, and the jello's jiggling." Many things in life also come to the point when they are out of reach. We need to be good stewards of the opportunities that are ours before we come to that point.

The Christmas Surprise

It was the fall of 1956, and I had a hankering for hamsters. When I was growing up, the arrival of the Sears & Roebuck Christmas catalog marked the beginning of the most wonderful season of the year. My mom asked us to look through the catalog and let her know what we wanted. One year the catalog featured hamsters. The noble qualities of hamsters were praised to high heaven. They were described as being good pets that rapidly reproduced. I began to consider how I could raise dozens of hamsters, sell them to all of my friends, and become the hamster king of the Western hemisphere. Although I had never actually seen a hamster, I decided that this was the present that I wanted. I told my mother, who received the

news with, what I thought, was a less than an enthusiastic expression.

While we often told our mom what kind of present
we wanted, it was never a sure thing that we would get
it. In the end, the exact present(s) that we got was still
a surprise. So, in the days leading up to Christmas that
year, I was filled with a great sense of anticipation over
whether I would actually receive the Christmas "surprise"
and enter into the joys of being a genuine hamster owner.

My grandmother and uncle, Mixon (who was un-
married at the time), lived about a mile down the road
from us. Often the shipment from Sears & Roebuck was
dropped off at their house and held in safekeeping until
Christmas arrived to keep it away from our prying eyes. I
hesitate to call Mixon The Grinch Who Stole Christmas,
but he took inordinate pleasure in poking holes in our
Christmas expectations.

About a week before Christmas that year, he and my
grandmother came to the house for a visit. When he saw
me, he said, "When are you going to come down to the
house and get your rats?"

That's when I knew that I was getting hamsters. I didn't
know whether to be happy about the hamsters, mad at
Mixon for calling them rats, or disappointed that there
was no longer any element of surprise left for Christmas
morning. We have always loved surprises. They give life
zest and excitement, but now at least part of the surprise

was gone. There was, however, still a surprise awaiting me on Christmas morning.

When my brothers and I got up on Christmas morning, we went sprinting into the cold living room before a fire had been built in the fireplace, and there were my long-awaited hamsters. They looked just like they did in the Sears & Roebuck Christmas catalog. But then, that's when I discovered another surprise. My mom and dad had gotten me a new reversible coat for the winter of 1956-57. I never did like to get clothes for Christmas. I figured that my parents were required by law to buy me a coat. Christmas was the time to get something they weren't obligated to give me. On this occasion, however, I understood that a good practical gift like a coat sort of balanced out the impractical gift of the hamsters.

Here was the surprise; in arranging the gifts the night before, my parents had laid the coat across the end of the hamster cage. During the night, the hamsters, in an effort to make their bed warmer in the cold living room, had looked around for some bedding material and had found my new coat on top of the cage. They had eaten a massive hole in the shoulder of my new coat and had lined their beds with the material. Fortunately, the coat was reversible, but I never got to reverse it since I had a large hamster hole that had been taken out of one side of the coat. The coat looked okay on the good side, but I always got a little chilly on one shoulder when I wore it.

The thing with the hamsters never worked out as I had anticipated. They never reproduced. I don't know who the matchmaker was at Sears Roebuck, but the two of them hated each other and did a lot fighting. But, I'll tell you this; that Christmas was surrounded by surprises because of them.

There has always been a note of surprise about Christmas. That was true of the first Christmas—the Messiah was born, not to royalty in Judea in the capital city of Jerusalem, but in the little village of Bethlehem to a poor young couple from Nazareth up in Galilee. Can you imagine that—Nazareth was a town that had a reputation for being one from which no good thing ever came. Although Jesus came from the realms of glory, He was born in a stable and laid in a manger. That night angels made a surprise appearance to shepherds in a field outside of Bethlehem to tell them of the birth of this child, and the shepherds showed up at the stable for a visit. Within a week or more, wise men came from a far country to see Him and to present Him with valuable gifts. That first Christmas was filled with surprises!

It was a wonderful and surprising thing that happened on that first Christmas morning. Though most did not see, while we slept, God walked down the stairway of heaven with a baby in His arms. He placed among us the most sacred and precious gift of all. He gave us His Son. What an astounding thing to do! Jesus is the most beautiful and surprising gift that has ever been given at Christmas!

The Dry Seasons of Life

In 1971, Danielle and I lived in Southeast Texas at Burkeville, where I served as pastor of Burkeville Baptist Church. In the summer of that year, Bro. Sam Farris, the Director of East Texas Baptist Encampment near Newton, Texas, invited Danielle to direct the GA Camp for girls at the encampment. Danielle and I had a deal that if they invited her to direct a camp, they had to invite me to be the camp pastor. So, since they really wanted her to direct the camp, they reluctantly took me as camp pastor. We started the camp on Monday morning, and we had a good group of girls—about 100 or more. Each morning we would have a worship service, and a little missionary lady who served in Africa had a mission time with the girls. By mid-week, we had settled into a routine, and everything was going great.

On Wednesday night of that week, Danielle and I had made our final round of the campground, had chased the last campers back into their cabins, and had settled down for the night. About 2:00 AM, there was a knock on our door, and it was Bro. Sam Farris. Bro. Sam told me that I had a call over in the camp office. It was in the days before cell phones (remember those?), so I got dressed and went to the office to take the call.

I had not been in the ministry very long, but I had been in it long enough to know that phone calls at 2:00 o'clock in the morning never bring any good news. I picked up the phone, and it was my older brother Wayne. Wayne said, "Lynn, Daddy died tonight."

My dad was young, only 58 years old, but he had a lot of health problems and had been bedridden for a couple of years. Still, the news of his death was a shock to us. Danielle and I packed our bags and left for Louisiana in the middle of the night to be with our family. We stayed there for the funeral and for several more days before returning to Burkeville.

After we had been home for a few days, there was a knock on the door. I answered it, and it was the little missionary who had been with us at camp. I invited her in, and she came in, carrying a paper sack in her hand. She expressed her sympathy to us in the loss of my father. She told me how upset the girls had been to hear about his death, and that they had prayed for us throughout the week. I told her how much that meant to us.

Then she took the paper sack that she had brought, reached inside, and brought out two long, beautiful cow horns that had been carved into two birds, standing with their beaks straight up in the air. She said, "I want you to have these. In Africa where I serve, these are the birds that come to us in the dry season." I thanked her for such a wonderful gift. We visited a few minutes more, and then she left.

It has been many years since my father died, and since that little missionary gave me that gift. I still have those two beautiful horns on top of a bookcase in my office, and I see them every day. And every time that I see them, I thank God. I thank Him that He is a God who comes to us in the dry seasons of life! He is Immanuel, God with us, and I am overwhelmed by His comforting and sustaining presence!

The Fruit of Self-Control

Each summer a significant event occurs. The sun, which begins its slow journey northward in December, reaches the northern limits of its journey on June 21. It arrives at 23 ½ degrees north of the equator, pauses briefly over the Tropic of Cancer, and then abruptly turns and begins its journey southward again. The day of the sun's northernmost advance, the summer solstice, is our longest day of the year. After that, our time of daylight slowly begins to shorten. As a gardener, I greet the day with a certain sadness, knowing that the growing season is on the decline.

You would expect that June 21, the longest day of the year, would be our hottest day, given the fact that we have more hours of sunshine that day than any other day.

But, as you know, that is not the case. Our hottest days of the summer generally come in July or August. Why is that so? The reason is that there is a slow build-up of heat during the summer. It is the cumulative effect of many days of longer sunshine that causes our hemisphere to become like a pressure cooker that gradually collects the heat. The same is true on any given day. The hottest time of the day is not at noon when the sun is the highest. It is in the afternoon when the heat of the day has been compounded by more hours of heating.

Sometimes it is like that in life. Anger, irritation, and frustration tend to build in our lives. Often it is not a single big incident that pushes us to the boiling point. It is the cumulative effect of many incidents. If we allow these to collect and do not process them as they occur, then they may push our emotional temperatures to all-time highs.

Collecting is a popular hobby. People collect all kinds of things. They collect stamps, coins, autographs, and baseball cards. Unfortunately, some also collect resentments, grudges, and old scores not settled. When this collection reaches enormous proportions, it can lead to devastating results.

Heywood Heil-Broun once said, "It has been my experience in the shower that the hot water is often difficult to get started and even harder to turn off." Anger and hatred are like that.

Each year on pitching mounds across the nation, pitchers ply their trade. Major League pitchers can throw fastballs that reach 100 mph. Some pitchers can throw that fast who never make the Major Leagues. The reason why they never make it? They lack control. It doesn't matter how fast you can throw the ball, if you can't control it, then you can't play in the majors.

That's the way it is in life. You may have exceptional abilities, but unless you have control, then you can never be all that God wants you to be. God can help. Paul said, "The fruit of the Spirit is love, joy, peace, longsuffering, . . . self-control" (Gal. 5:22-23). Let Him help you! Ask Him for the fruit of self-control.

The importance of a Transmission

One of the critical parts of an automobile is the transmission. Located in the car is a powerful engine designed to produce a great deal of horsepower. But if this power is to be of any value, it must make contact with the drive wheels, which help the car move. This is where the transmission comes in. The job of the transmission is to transmit the power of the engine to the drive wheels. It helps make a difference where the rubber meets the road. A beautiful automobile with a powerful engine that merely sits and roars is of little value.

The Christian life is like that. We have a dynamic source of power within us, but unless that power is transmitted to the practical areas of living it amounts to little. That has always been a problem with the people of God. We have often seen our responsibility as that of being filled with the power of God and talking about His indwelling presence, but then doing little or nothing as a result.

The philosopher Voltaire was critical of some of his contemporaries who did a lot of talking but then never did anything about their beliefs. He said that they were like an oven that was always heating up but never actually cooked anything. The value of an oven is not in the amount of heat that it produces, but in the amount of food that it produces. Sooner or later our words must find their way into concrete action.

A recurring theme of Scripture is the call to deeds instead of mere words. Samuel told Saul that what God really wanted out of him was obedience, not sacrifice (1 Sam. 15:22). Micah once asked rhetorically, "What does God want out of us? Does He want elaborate sacrifices and rich gifts? No," he responded, "God wants us to act justly and to love mercy and to walk humbly with our God" (Micah 6:8). May God give us the grace to translate our faith into action.

The Joys and the Challenges of the Seasons of Life

When I lived in Booneville, Mississippi, my neighbor for 17 years was Bob Taylor. Bob was a creative sort of guy with many interests. He was head of the Music Department at Northeast Mississippi Community College and in his spare time served at the time as Minister of Music for the First United Methodist Church in Corinth. Bob's interests and creativity did not extend, however, to his yard. By his own admission, he was utterly uninterested in it. His wife Jan tried various ways to encourage him to become more interested in the yard, but all of her efforts met with little success.

I, on the other hand, enjoyed working in my yard. It was a perfect change of pace for me. I encountered some opposition from my neighbor Bob, however, because he said that my yard was putting too much pressure on him. He would amble across the street on occasion and try to talk me into slacking off a little bit.

I didn't see much of Bob in the winter because I was not out in the yard much. I hunkered down around the fireplace trying to survive the cold and waiting for the first sign of spring and a chance to pursue my hobby again. One time during the winter I ran into Bob, and he had a big smile on his face. He said, "I love winter! Winter is the great leveler. I love it because in winter all the yards are brown and dead and look exactly alike. You can't tell who works in their yard and who doesn't."

Well, I suppose Bob and I both needed the winter season. Winter is a season that requires a change of pace and different activities. There is something that is healthy about that.

In his book, Travels with Charley, John Steinbeck said that living in a good climate year-round bored him to death. He asked, "How can one know color in perpetual green, and what good is warmth without cold to give it sweetness?"

It is this variation of the seasons that makes us appreciate the distinct qualities of each. Charles Swindoll said, "I am glad God changes the times and the seasons. Just think how dull things would become if He didn't paint nature's scenes in different colors several times a year."

Not only does the year come with its distinct seasons, but so does life. I suppose if we had to choose, we'd always want joy and happiness. Instead, life comes with its difficult times and its times of pain. While we do not relish them, such experiences make us appreciate the times of joy and blessing more than ever.

The name of Swindoll's book on the subject is Growing Strong in the Seasons of Life. That's what our prayer should be—that God will help us grow strong in the experiences of the changing seasons of life.

The Ministry of Affirmation

When you were a child, do you remember receiving stars by your name for some noteworthy accomplishment? I can remember those big shiny gold stars beside my name when I was a "Beginner" in Sunday School. We got one for every Sunday that we attended. No General in the Army took more pride in his medals than I did in those gold stars.

Recently I heard on the radio about a modern version of those gold stars. Chrissa Palmer is a woman who lives in Charlotte, North Carolina. Some time ago she went on the offensive to encourage and reward outstanding behavior. She carries some colored stars in her purse, and when she sees persons doing something positive, she gives them a star.

For instance, she said that she was in the grocery store recently as people jockeyed for position to get to the check-out registers. A woman struggling with an armload of groceries and a small child approached one of the registers. There was one man in front of her. When he saw her struggle, he insisted that she get in front of him. When Chrissa Palmer saw that, she went over to the man and said, "I saw what you did, and I think it was great." With that, she reached into her purse, took out a bright, shiny star, and placed it on the lapel of his coat. She said that in all of the years that she has chosen to recognize persons for their deeds of kindness, no one has ever refused to take a star.

The ministry of encouragement and affirmation is a worthy ministry to enter. People around us need encouragement when they are doing something right. It is interesting to notice how Jesus walked through life. He paused to call attention to a poor widow who cast a single penny into the offering box at the Temple. He said, "She has given more than anyone." He was always noticing and affirming folks who did the right thing. We all need encouragement and affirmation. How about handing out a few gold stars this week?

The Ministry of Encouragement

Someone has said that we ought to be as resilient as a golf ball that is dropped onto a cement floor. The golf ball rebounds from such a drop with amazing resilience. It bounces back as high or higher than the point from which it was dropped. One of the problems is that life comes with repeated disappointments that tend to take the resilience out of us. After another loss on the baseball field, Linus told Charlie Brown, "Charlie Brown, don't be discouraged. That's the way life is. You win some, and you lose some." Charlie responded, "That would be nice."

Life often comes with more than its share of difficulties and defeats. In fact, when you read the Bible you discover that many persons of faith were overwhelmed by the problems they faced. Moses went on his mission to

Egypt in response to God's command. The opposition of the Pharaoh was so fierce that Moses was overwhelmed. He complained that God had not rescued His people at all like He had promised.

Elijah ran for his life before Jezebel. When he ran as far as he could go, he prayed that he might die. He said, "I have had enough, Lord" (1 Kings 19:4).

God called a reluctant Jeremiah to go on a mission for Him. Things did not work out as Jeremiah had anticipated. There were no converts—only rejection and downright persecution. Jeremiah complained to God: "O Lord, you deceived me, and I was deceived." He complained, "Cursed be the day I was born." He wanted to escape. He said, "Oh that I had in the wilderness a lodging place of wayfaring men; that I might leave my people and go from them!"

Moses, Elijah, and Jeremiah—three great men of God, but all of them suffered through times of overwhelming disappointment and discouragement. It is part of our human condition. Faith in God, even great faith, does not put us off-limits to its reach.

One of the greatest things that we can do as a family of faith is to offer to each other the gift of encouragement. The English word "encourage" is derived from two Latin words meaning "to put the heart into." That's what encouragement does—to those who are disheartened it puts the heart back into them.

When all the cars leave the church parking lot on Sunday morning after worship, sometimes there is one car that is left—someone's battery is dead. What happens then is that someone comes alongside that car with jumper cables and jumpstarts the engine. Soon they are on their way. I would like to think that in some far greater way something like that has occurred in our worship service that day. The writer of Hebrews said, "Let us not give up meeting together, as some are in the habit of doing, but let us encourage one another" (Heb. 10:24).

The Power and Demand of a Vision

May 3, 1947, marked the beginning of a massive undertaking. On that date, Korzak Ziolkowski arrived in the Black Hills of South Dakota to accept an invitation from Native American leaders to carve a statue of the great chief Crazy Horse. Ziolkowski fashioned a model of Crazy Horse astride a stallion with tossing head. The model depicted the chief pointing with his left hand to the distant horizon.

Now, where would Ziolkowski carve the sculpture and what would be the size of it? The sculptor chose a granite mountain 17 miles southwest of Mount Rushmore. He envisioned, emerging from the mountain, a sculpture, which would be 563 feet high and 641 feet long. The completed sculpture would be the world's largest.

Work on the project began in 1948 and is still going on. Ziolkowski himself died in 1982 at the age of 74. Among his final words to his family was a charge to finish the work on Crazy Horse. His family has been faithful to that charge. The face of Crazy Horse is now complete and stands 90 feet high. Work on the project has now been going on for many years, and many more years of work remain before its completion.

Big projects are inspiring. They make you think big thoughts. That's the way it is when you look at a mountain being reshaped. Vision is one of those big thoughts. It takes vision to look at a mountain and see a sculpture emerge.

When booking rooms for a vacation, you will discover that a place "with a view" is valued more highly than other places. Even more valuable is a life "with a view"— persons who can see things, persons who have visions of what can be. If something big is to be accomplished, faith is a necessity. Jesus said that if you have faith enough, you can move a mountain. Still, it takes a lot of faith to tackle such a mountain and begin chipping away to refashion it into a sculpture.

Sometimes we give lip service to the power of faith to move mountains, but in our lives, we never tackle any specific mountains. We generalize our faith.

Genuine faith can lead to significant accomplishments. A champion high jumper explained how he was able to jump so high. He said, "I take my heart and throw it over the bar, and then I jump after it." Life can be transformed by such a leap of faith.

In order to accomplish something big, endurance is needed. You don't transform a mountain into a sculpture overnight. The same is true of life. Jesus said that before a person begins to build a tower, he ought to sit down and count the cost. If he does not calculate the cost, he may leave behind a half-completed tower. The problem with many of us is that our lives are littered with half-completed projects. The world is full of starters, but it's the finishers who count. I challenge you to finish what you have started for Christ.

The Power of Your Influence

I heard about two gas company employees, a senior training supervisor and a young trainee, who were checking gas meters in a suburban neighborhood. They parked their truck on the street and walked up a driveway to a house. Once there, they opened the back gate and went into the yard to check the gas meter. As the two were checking the gas meter, a little senior adult woman was peering at them through her kitchen window.

As the two were leaving the yard, the senior supervisor told his younger coworker that he thought he was in better shape even though he was older. To prove his point, he challenged the younger man to a footrace down the driveway to their truck. As the two men were running as hard as they could toward the truck, suddenly the little senior adult lady passed both of them as though they were standing still.

When the two men arrived at the truck, they stopped and asked the woman, who was standing out in the street, what was wrong. Gasping for breath, she said, "When I saw two gas men running away from my house as fast as you two were running, I figured that I had better run too."

You must never underestimate the power of your influence. When people observe what you are doing, the impact of what you are doing can have a powerful effect on them.

In fact, it is often the power of our unconscious influence that has the greatest effect on people. In the Temple in Jerusalem, various people came to give their offerings to God. Some wanted to call attention to the large sums of money that they were giving. In contrast to these, there was a poor widow who slipped into the Temple and threw into the offering box one "mite." She was not trying to influence anyone by her giving. She was giving out of a heart of love.

What the widow did not know was that Jesus was watching. He called all of His disciples together and told them about the widow's offering. While it was but a "mite" she threw into the box, Jesus said that it was "all her living." The influence of that sacrificial gift given by one poor widow has influenced Christian givers for centuries. You never can tell what kind of influence your life will have on other people.

Albert Schweitzer left a career as a great organist in Europe to enroll in medical school and become a doctor. After becoming a physician, he then went to Africa where he invested the remaining years of his life in ministering to the poor. His example of sacrifice and giving captivated a generation of people.

Norman Cousins once said of Schweitzer, "The greatness of Schweitzer was not so much what he did for others, but what others have done because of him and the power of his example. This is the real measure of the man."

In a sense, that is the real measure of all of us. It's not just what we do, but what we influence others to do. What kind of influence is your life having on people around you?

The Still Small Voice of Conscience

One of my first encounters with abstract theological thought came when I was very small. I was listening to a conversation that my mom and dad were having about a person's "conscience." They were discussing whether a "conscience" was a reliable guide for life. I remember the wonder that I felt in hearing a big word like "conscience." I had never heard the word before, and I was not sure what a "conscience" was. I was not sure whether I had one or not.

I heard of a small boy who was asked if he knew what a "conscience" was. He said, "Yes, a conscience is what makes you tell your mother what you did before your sister tells her." In my case, it was what made me tell my mother when all threats to my little brother showed no signs of deterring him from telling her.

Actually, conscience is the inner voice that is continuously monitoring our actions and inactions. It is like the voice of a judge who is constantly pronouncing "guilty" or "not guilty" over our lives.

One of the problems of this inner judge is that he is not very reliable. Sometimes he abdicates his role and allows things to slip by that really should be condemned. Sometimes his voice is so muted that it is drowned out in the rabble of other voices around us. What we often need is to be quiet long enough to hear this inner voice.

Someone has suggested another possibility. The suggestion is that what we need most in life is an inventor who will create a device for amplifying the still, small voice of conscience. Even if such a device could be invented, however, merely hearing the voice of conscience would not solve the problem of the reliability of this voice. How much can you depend upon it to give proper guidance for your life?

Given our sinful nature, it is sure that this inner voice has been distorted by sin like every other part of our being. How can we make it more reliable? One thing that we can do is spend time in the presence of God in worship and prayer. William Templeton gave a classic definition of worship. The first part of that definition declares, "Worship is the submission of all our nature to God. It is the quickening of conscience by His holiness." Such exposure to God makes conscience considerably more reliable.

Another way to strengthen the reliability of conscience is by exposure to the truth of the Word of God. In the midst of a great testing experience, Martin Luther declared, "My conscience is captive to the Word of God." As we study the Word, this Word comes to sensitize the conscience and make it a more reliable and dynamic voice within us.

Is conscience a reliable guide? Not inherently. It needs continued exposure to the light of God's presence to increase its reliability.

True Grit

When I was growing up in Plainview, Louisiana, jobs for a boy were scarce. You could pick cotton or peas for the neighbors, but that was a very seasonal activity (And if you were a slow picker like I was, there was not much money in it). But then there was always the lure of selling the Grit newspaper. My older brother Wayne had sold Grit for a while but had soon given it up. I was sure that I could be a success.

I signed on for the job of delivering the weekly paper and ordered 28 copies. The selling price for Grit was 10 cents. Of that amount, I got to keep 4 cents, and I sent the other 6 cents to Grit each week. One of the problems of selling newspapers in the country was that the houses were so far apart. Not only were they far apart, but also they were located on dirt roads, which had deep sand beds and high hills. That made pumping a bicycle with 28 newspapers on board somewhat difficult. More daunting than the hills and the sand beds, however, were the dogs that lurked under porches and behind buildings. The people on my route were always friendly, paid cash up front, and sometimes offered water or other forms of refreshment. In spite of that, spending every Friday afternoon and Saturday morning carrying Grit got a little old.

I've always wondered why the editors chose the name "Grit" for their newspaper. Probably it was named that because it was a collection of short articles about the nitty-gritty business of life. On the other hand, the word "grit" can also mean perseverance, stamina, sticking-with-it. The editors may have been trying to send a message to their young employees across the country. They knew the job was not easy and the pay was small. What their newspaper salesmen needed was "grit."

I think there is something to be said about the importance of "grit" in life in general and in the Christian life in particular. I would like to tell you that the Christian life is filled with one thrill after another. The truth of the matter is that the Christian life does have its thrills, but it also has its long, difficult stretches that make many demands of you. I must confess that after several months of heat, hills, sand, and dogs, I became a Grit dropout. In the larger matter of faith, I pray that God will help me continue to stick with it.

Unifying the Church

There was an unusual incident that took place in a small town in 1966. The local church had problems. It was divided, and the pastor was looking for a way to unite the church and to energize it. About this time the church building burned to the ground. The fire looked suspicious and an investigation was begun. Everything uncovered in the investigation pointed to arson. Not only did the investigation point to arson, but it also pointed to the pastor as the one who was guilty of the arson. Upon being questioned by the authorities, the pastor admitted his guilt. When asked for an explanation, he said, "They needed a project to unify them."

I have seen a lot of programs come along over the years. A lot of these have promised to energize and unify the church. Until this incident, however, I had never heard of the Church Arson Program.

The matter of unifying and energizing the church has always been a challenge. Perhaps that should come as no surprise given the membership requirements of the church. The church is the only organization in the world in which membership is based on the qualification that the candidate be unworthy of membership. Given the fact that we all are sinners—forgiven sinners, but still sinners—then forging unity is always a problem. The dynamic for genuine unity should come from the fact that the head of the church is Jesus Christ. As we look to Him for direction, we all can be moving in the same direction. We can also be unified by a commitment to the common tasks of sharing the gospel with the lost and ministering to the needs of people around us. Christ can give genuine unity to the church.

Vitamin "I"

I started taking vitamins at an early age. Before I could swallow a pill, Mom gave us "Vidaylin." Vidaylin was a syrupy liquid that contained vitamins in a liquid form. Some kids didn't like it, but I did. I was all for anything that had a sweet taste.

Under Mom's watchful eye and persistent prodding, I later graduated to vitamins in pill form. To this day, I take several vitamins each day. I'm not sure I need all these vitamins, but if I don't take them, I feel that I am betraying my mother and the way she raised me.

Of course, I am aware of the dangers of taking mega-doses of vitamins, and I avoid doing that. In fact, the other day I read of a particular danger related to vitamins and the Christian life. The danger is an overdose of vitamin "I."

There was a man in the New Testament who suffered from a classic case of an overdose of vitamin "I." He was a Pharisee who stood at the temple and prayed "about himself: God 'I' thank you that "I" am not like other men . . . 'I' fast twice a week and give a tenth of all 'I' get" (Luke 18:11-12).

A mega-dose of vitamin 'I' has all kinds of harmful effects on our spiritual health. It causes us always to be maneuvering to get affirmation from others. In the words of Calvin Miller, we spend too much time "fishing for compliments at the deep piers of ego."

It causes us to begin to take credit and praise that rightly only belong to God. A. W. Tozer imagined how it may have been when Jesus came riding the donkey into Jerusalem on Palm Sunday. The street was thronged with people who were waving palm branches and singing songs of praise. Tozer said, "I wonder if the donkey thought all the shouts of praise were for him?"

Maybe that is the particular problem of preachers, teachers, and others who serve the Lord. We are around the Lord and sometimes think the praise is for us instead of the Lord whom we try to present.

An overdose of vitamin "I" will cause us to take far too much credit and give too little credit to God. Some persons even tout themselves as being "self-made-men." The problem with a "self-made-man" is that he worships his creator instead of the God of all creation.

An overdose of vitamin "I" causes us to feel self-sufficient and to spurn the need for grace. W. E. Sangster had this advice on the subject. He said, "Pride is the first and worst of sins. On your way to ask for the mercy of God, it will tug at your sleeve and try to dissuade you. Brush it aside."

Finish your journey. Make your way to the foot of the cross. Acknowledge your need for the grace of God and of having the persistent problem of overdosing on vitamin "I".

What Happens When You Goof Up?

Several years ago, I put in a drip watering system for all of my outdoor plants. They've thought of everything with this system, including some small devices to cover your mistakes. If you goof up and punch a hole in the supply line at the wrong spot, they have included what they call "goof plugs." Stick a goof plug into the misplaced hole, and the mistake is corrected.

Now I do not know who invented this system, but I've got to appreciate their allowance for the human variable. They know that regardless of how clear the instructions are, or how careful the installer is, someone is still going to goof up. Thank heavens for a designer who understands such things.

I am also grateful for others who have recognized that foible in human nature. We owe the development of rubber to those who sought some device to erase a mistake made with a pencil. They discovered that they could make this material and put it on the other end of the pencil to "rub" out the mistake; hence, the name "rubber." They later discovered that the substance had other applications as well.

Movement from pencils to pen and typewriters occasioned harder erasers and eventually "liquid paper" and "correct type." Now those have been replaced by a nice "delete" key on the computer, which does the job before the print goes on the paper.

Unfortunately, in the larger area of our mistakes in life, people are often not very forgiving. They never let you forget the sins that you've committed.

The good news is that God is much more forgiving than that. Even when we goof up and fail miserably, He does not write us off. His love and forgiveness are available. "If we confess our sins, he is faithful and just to forgive us our sins and to cleanse us from all unrighteousness" (1 John 1:9). You can trust Him for that today!

When It Rains on the Just and the Unjust

West Texas is notorious for its dry climate. A tourist was passing through the Texas Panhandle one hot August day when he stopped to get some gas in a small West Texas town. As the man pumped the gas, he looked out over the dry, barren landscape that shimmered through the afternoon heat waves. When he paid for his gas, he asked the attendant if it ever rained very much out there. The attendant drawled, "Nope." "Well, tell me," the tourist said, "what is the biggest rain that you've ever gotten out here?" The old Texan responded, "Do you remember Noah's flood? Well, we got half an inch that time."

When I served as pastor in Booneville, Mississippi, we got considerably more rain than that. In fact, on Friday through Saturday, October 12-13, 2001, according to my rain gauge, we got 6.5 inches of rain. According to scientists, one inch of rain means that 65,000 tons, or more than 15 million gallons of water, falls on each square mile. Booneville has within its city limits roughly 99 square miles. This means that during those two days there fell on our fair city about 9.6 billion gallons of water or more than 418 million tons of water.

How would you like to get a bill for that much water? At $1.50 per thousand gallons, that would mean a water bill of about 14.6 million dollars. That would put a strain on the old city budget, wouldn't it?

Of course, the good news is that God did not send us a bill for the water. It was His gift to us. We did nothing to deserve it, but it was given to us anyway.

I also noticed that the rain fell on everyone in town. Jesus said that is the way it would come. "For [God] sends rain on the just and on the unjust" (Matt. 5:45). He loves everyone, not just those who love Him in return. His hope is that as He continues to shower His love upon all of us eventually everyone will respond to His gracious love.

Predicting exactly when it will rain and how much it will rain is a tricky business. One old farmer told a friend that you could tell if it is going to rain by observing the cows in the field. If the cows were lying down, it was not going to rain. If they were standing up, it was going to rain. His friend passed by his field a few days later wondering whether it would rain. He looked at the cows and then went and told the farmer, "Half of your cows are lying down and half of them are standing up. Now what does that mean?" The old farmer said, "It means half of them are wrong."

There are a good many things in this world that are still controlled by God. When it rains and how much it rains are two of those things. We exhibit some degree of maturity when we are willing to accept God's plan and control in life.

Working on Your Vocabulary

Recently I've heard a commercial on the radio about how to have a great vocabulary. According to the commercial, a poor vocabulary is very harmful. A poor vocabulary can cause others to question your background, education, and even your intelligence. In order to alleviate this problem, you are encouraged to send money for a computer program which can teach you 100 new, impressive words that can immediately assure you of a great future.

Reminds me of a Bill Thorn story. Jack was home from college visiting his folks in their little mountain cabin. As he sat in the front room with his father, he said, "May I tell you a narrative?" His father asked, "What on earth is a narrative, son?" Jack replied, "A narrative is a tale."

Later that evening, just before bedtime, Jack said to his father, "May I extinguish the light?" His father said, "What do you mean by saying 'extinguish'?" Jack replied, "It means 'to put out.'"

The next evening Jack's fiancé and her family came to meet his family. Jack's father wanted very much to make a good impression on these important visitors. Halfway through the evening, the old dog walked into the cabin and stretched out on the floor. Jack's father raised his voice and said, "Jack, will you please take the dog by the narrative and extinguish him!"

Vocabularies are important. They say something about us. All of us ought to work on them, especially Christians. I'll tell you a word that ought to mark our vocabularies. It is the word "love." We live in a world that communicates with words and actions that are often abrupt and abrasive. The one who is the most skilled in such tactics is the one who gets his way. Often it is self-interest that calls the shots in our lives. A billboard proclaimed this message: "Yes, I'd like to help you out. Show me how you came in."

The Christian is under the mandate of Christ to come at it from a different angle. It is the angle of love. Jesus said, "By this shall all people know that you are my disciples—if you have love for one another."

Or, it may be that we need to dust off another old word—"forgiveness." A seven-year-old girl wrote this letter to God. She said, "Dear God: We studied in Sunday

School that we should love our enemies. I am only six, and I do not have any enemies yet. I hope to have some by the time I am seven. Love, Jennifer." Jennifer probably does not need to worry about such a detail. Given time and the nature of things, she will have more enemies than she needs in a few years. The antidote for such a process is forgiveness. Paul wrote, "Be kind and compassionate to one another, forgiving each other, just as in Christ God forgave you."

Love and forgiveness—now there is the beginning of a great vocabulary!

Your Best Years

A visitor in a home noticed two pairs of bronzed baby shoes on a shelf in the den. Knowing that the couple had two teenage daughters, the visitor said, "I see that you bronzed the girls' baby shoes." "Yes," the father said, "wish now that I'd kept the shoes and bronzed the girls."

Ever feel that way? Have you ever wanted to stop time in motion, preserve a child at some particularly lovable age? When would it be? When she was a baby and totally dependent on you? When he was three and was convinced that you knew everything in the world?

We not only want to do that with people; we also want to do that with moments. We look back on golden (bronze) moments that we would like to hold onto forever. One of the problems, of course, is that as time progresses, we tend to idealize the past. We remember golden moments and forget the downside of every time. A baby is lovable but also makes 24-hour-a-day demands of you. A three-year-old may think that you know everything but is not convinced that he ought to do it your way.

When we are living through such moments, we often are far more impressed with the negative than the positive. Only later do we see the positive side.

Martin Marty summarized a short story by Willa Cather entitled Our Best Years (intriguing title, isn't it?). In the story, an older woman reflects, "Well, this I know; our best years are when we're working hardest and going right ahead when we can hardly see our way out." Marty added, "I think similar thoughts when I look back on my years as a pastor, a parent of a young family, and a struggling young professor."

When are our best years? Our best years are not years that are devoid of challenge or struggle. Our best years are when we are engaged in struggle and challenge as we try to accomplish something important. Who knows? With God's help and your cooperation, this could be your best year.

CPSIA information can be obtained
at www.ICGtesting.com
Printed in the USA
FSHW04n0005310318
46083FS